Colin Pomeroy was born and brought up in Weymouth and joined the Air Training Corps as soon as he was old enough to. Aged 16, he was awarded a flying scholarship and held a private pilot's licence before he held a car driver's licence.

He joined the Royal Air Force in 1960, and flew initially on Shackleton aircraft and then for ten years on the Nimrod, in the UK and, literally, around the world. He retired in 1980 as a Squadron Leader, his last sortie being a flypast at that year's Weymouth Carnival, and the following year joined Orion Airways flying Boeing 737 aircraft to destinations throughout Europe, the Mediterranean and North Africa.

He retired in 1989 on medical grounds, but maintained his interest in aviation for many years, most especially by his involvement in the Air Training Corps. With nearly 11,500 accident-free flying hours in his log books, he still enjoys the occasional light aircraft flight in Dorset skies.

A Vice President of the Society of Dorset Men, Editorial Board member for *The Military Times* and an Honorary Vice President of the Poole Flying Boats Celebration, Colin has written extensively on military history, aviation, transportation and Dorset, especially Weymouth. He now lives in North Devon.

IN THE SAME SERIES

DORSET: The Army
George Forty

DORSET: The Royal Navy
Stuart Morris

FOLLOWING PAGE
Spitfire pilots of No 234 Squadron at rest in the pilots' room at RAF Warmwell, 26 July 1941. The Squadron had spent much of its time in the West Country, flying convoy patrols and bomber escorts to the French ports (IWM CH 3430).

DORSET
THE ROYAL AIR FORCE

COLIN POMEROY

THE DOVECOTE PRESS

Weapons Week 1941. Two flights from RAF Warmwell march across
Weymouth's Westham Bridge. Universal (Bren Gun) Carriers
bring up the rear.

First published in 2011 by The Dovecote Press Ltd
Stanbridge, Wimborne Minster, Dorset BH21 4JD

ISBN 978-1-904-34981-5

Typeset in FS Ingrid and designed by The Dovecote Press Ltd
Printed and bound by GraphyCems, Navarra

All papers used by The Dovecote Press are natural, recyclable products
made from wood grown in sustainable, well-managed forests.

A CIP catalogue record for this book is available from the British Library

CONTENTS

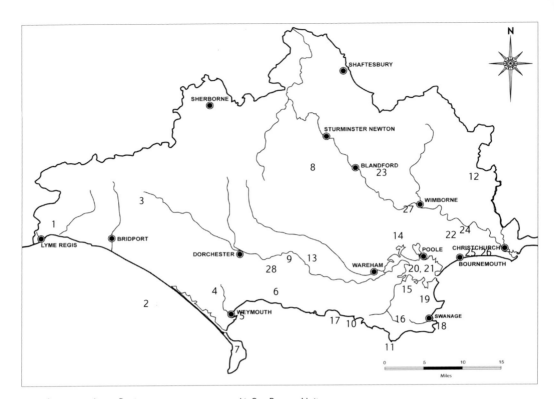

1	Lyme Regis	Air Sea Rescue Unit
2	Lyme Bay	Bombing and Gunnery Ranges
3	Toller	Airship Mooring Station
4	Chickerell	Airstrip, Bombing Ranges Unit
5	Weymouth	Air Sea Rescue Unit, Range Maintenance Vessels Base
6	Ringstead	Radar, Troposcatter Station
7	Portland	West Cliff, East Cliff and Portland (Rotor) Radars
8	Bulbarrow Hill	GEE Station
9	Warmwell	Airfield
10	Kimmeridge	Mandrel
11	Worth Matravers	Radar, Airstrip, Radar Research Establishment, Training Units
12	Three Legged Cross	Decoy Site
13	Moreton	Airship Mooring Station
14	Upton	Airship Mooring Station
15	Godlingston Hill	Radio Monitoring and Deception Unit
16	Acton	Ping Pong
17	Brandy Bay	GEE Monitoring Base, Reserve GEE Transmitter
18	Tilly Whim	Oboe
19	Ballard Down	Gunnery Range
20	Hamworthy	Flying Boat Base
21	Poole	Air Sea Rescue Unit
22	Winton	Airfield
23	Tarrant Rushton	Airfield
24	Hurn	Airfield
25	Christchurch	Airfield, Shadow Factory
26	Southbourne	Radar
27	Wimborne Minster	Diathermy Machine
28	West Knighton Woods	Decoy Site

ONE

THE EARLY YEARS

The Royal Air Force, the world's very first independent air force, was formed on 1 April 1918 by the amalgamation of the Army's Royal Flying Corps (RFC) and the Royal Navy's Royal Naval Air Service (RNAS), the latter service bequeathing to the RAF 2,949 aircraft and some 5,378 officers and 49,688 men. Prior to this date the predominantly over-water nature of its role meant that the vast majority of military aviation in Dorset was under the control of the Royal Navy (see DORSET, The Royal Navy) and it was not until the 1920s and early 1930s that the RAF began to make its presence felt in the county, such as when the junior service's expanding maritime patrol squadrons began training visits to places such as Portland, Weymouth and Poole Harbour with graceful biplane flying boats like the Short Singapore, Supermarine Southampton and Saro London. It was only as the clouds of war gathered over Europe for the second time in the twentieth century, with the rise to power in Germany of Adolf Hitler, that the British Government awoke to the dangerously low strength of its armed forces in general, and the RAF – in terms of aircraft, modern all weather airfields and of support functions – in particular, and set out to rectify the situation, that

One of the most famous of all Royal Air Force photographs, the pilots of No 1 (Fighter) Squadron at their base in France on the day the Royal Air Force was formed, 1 April 1918.

the RAF began to appear in the county in any strength.

As the pages that follow reveal, the final years prior to the outbreak of war in September 1939 were a hive of aviation activity in Dorset: airfields sprang up, aircraft were posted in, ranges were activated, an Air Sea Rescue base became operational, and early warning radars and navigation aids came on line. Thanks to the forward thinking of politicians such as Winston Churchill, airmen such as Air Chief Marshal Hugh Dowding, the Air Officer Commanding Fighter Command, and, it has to be admitted, the breathing space gained by Prime Minister Neville Chamberlain at Munich in September 1938, Dorset was ready to earn its stripes in the dark days of the Battle of Britain through to the multitude variety of offensive operations which saw victory in Europe.

I hope that *DORSET, The Royal Air Force* will bring back proud memories to those who served in the RAF in our beautiful county during the years of the Second World War and in the anxious years of the Cold War that followed, and that those who were too young to wear the sovereign's light blue uniform will gain an appreciation of the seminal role that the Service played in the defence of the realm from the mid-1930s until the symbolic dismantling of the Berlin Wall in 1989 and the removal of the threat of inter-continental nuclear war. Dorset may be a nautical county; its skies, though, have also seen history written.

TWO

AIRSHIP MOORING STATIONS

During the Great War the threat to the nation of starvation due to heavy shipping losses from German U-boats was of the same magnitude as in the Second World War, but has received rather less prominence. To combat the U-boats the Admiralty established a series of mooring stations on the south and east coasts, operational control of the 'blimps' being co-ordinated with the activities of the Service's conventional, fixed-wing aircraft. The airships allocated were of the single-engined Sea Scout Zero class, quite capable machines for their time, which carried a crew of three and normally flew patrols of about 10 hours duration. Slow and vulnerable to strong winds, the airship – the first of which, *Mayfly*, entered service in 1909 – gave the fleet greatly extended visual range. A warship at sea level might only be able to see five or six miles to the horizon, whereas an airship (or, soon to follow, an aircraft) at some 5,000 feet above sea level can on a clear day see out to over ninety miles. Patrols were flown from the summer of 1917 until the war was over, until 31 March 1918 by the Royal Naval Air Service and from 1 April until the 11 November end of hostilities by the Royal Air Force.

Each site was equipped with a mooring mast located over a pit of large pit, the object of the pit being to allow the gondola and envelope of the Zero to be positioned for maintenance in a position of minimum wind resistance.

Sea Scout Zero class airship, with a non-rigid envelope of 143 feet in length and a volume of 70,000 cubic feet, was powered by a 75 horsepower Rolls Royce Hawk pusher engine and had a top speed of 53 mph. Each craft was capable of carrying a war load of two 110 pound bombs, plus a defensive Lewis machine gun.

UPTON

The airship sub-station at Upton was the easternmost of the three in the county and the first to be declared operational. It was located on the 913 acres Llewellin Estate, just to the west of Upton House, and was commissioned by the RNAS as a satellite station to the major airship base at Polegate, near Eastbourne in Sussex. Activated in 1917, it was transferred to RAF control in 1918 and, as did its companion station at Toller, continued to operate Sea Scout Zero class airships in the anti-submarine role under the control of Portsmouth Command until the Armistice, rapidly following which it was closed down. 100 acres of the former estate is now occupied by Upton Country Park.

TOLLER

A satellite sub-station to the Mullion base on the Lizard in Cornwall, Toller sub-station was constructed in the spring of 1918 and declared operational in time for its allocated airship to fly anti-submarine patrols in the Central English Channel by the summer. On 11 November 1918, when hostilities ceased and the carnage on the battlefields of Europe came to an end, the airship based at Toller was SSZ27, which was deflated in situ on 3 December when the site was de-activated prior to formal closure in January 1919.

MORETON

Also known locally as Woodsford, this was the last of the three airship sub-stations to be built in the county, being intended to bolster the thinly spread air coverage of the English Channel off the Dorset coastline. It never saw operational service and when hostilities drew to a close in November 1918 the final stages of construction were abruptly halted and the site abandoned. Had it been completed it would have had more of a permanent nature to it than either Upton or Toller, which is reflected in the fact that there are still buildings on the site in agricultural use today. Tragedy struck prior to the completion of the building works when a Belgium steel worker, Mr Paul Maupertuis, was killed when a gantry he was using to work on a fire escape on

Diagram showing the railway siding and platforms for the airship station at Moreton (Woodsford).

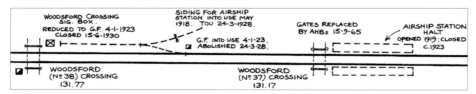

Having started life nearly 90 years ago as a crew room for the airship sub-station, this hut, together with two others of Second World War origin, still stands at Moreton today.

the observation tower gave way.

It is interesting to note from the diagram on the opposite page that there was a siding laid down by the railway for use by the airship station and a halt, with platforms on both the down and the up lines.

The land here was inspected in the mid-1930s by the Air Ministry as a possible site for an aerodrome, but its 350 or so acres were considered too restrictive and the airfield which later took the name RAF Warmwell was laid out just to the south and west, on the opposite side of the railway line between Waterloo and Weymouth.

THREE

AIRFIELDS

RAF CHRISTCHURCH

Flying having taken place earlier from a variety of strips in the very close vicinity, the airfield which was to become RAF Christchurch opened in February 1935 as Christchurch Airport and was host to a resident flying club and a number of fledgling airline companies, none of which was really a financial success until Great Western and Southern Air Lines began to make money from its services in 1939.

On the outbreak of the Second World War the airfield was closed down, but was requisitioned and reopened in April 1940 to house the Special Duties Flight (SDF) from RAF St Athan in South Wales, which moved to Hampshire, as it then was, to support the important research activities at the Telecommunications Research Establishment (TRE) at Worth Matravers. Aircraft on the SDF's charge included Avro Ansons, Fairey Battles, Bristol Blenheims and Handley Page Harrows, as well, later, as Hawker Hurricane Mk I L1592 which can be seen today at London's Science Museum – but in the guise of a No 615 Squadron aircraft. L1852 was one of three Hurricanes attached to the SDF, both as trials aircraft, when called for, and as close escorts to other less capable aircraft on charge. For a while a trio of Avro 504 biplanes of Great War lineage could also be seen at Christchurch where they carried out aero-tows of wooden gliders for TRE radar detection trials – evoking memories of the 1930s pleasure flights which were offered from the airfield by aviation pioneers such as Captain FC Fisher!

Towards the end of the summer an Anti-Aircraft Co-operation Unit moved in from Gosport, bringing more of the Fairey Battles to Christchurch. The airstrip had only grass runways, but the exceptionally fine weather of the summer of 1940 didn't put the drainage capability to the test.

Meanwhile, the Battle for France being over and with Nazi forces marshalling just across the Channel ready for an invasion, genuine worries were expressed about the vulnerability of the trials aircraft parked at Christchurch, so a dispersal strip was established at Sway in the New Forest.

At the same time as these other activities were going on work started in the north-east corner of the airfield on the construction of a Shadow Factory, a component in a scheme embarked upon as far back as 1936 to disperse aircraft production in an attempt to minimise the risk of a total collapse in manufacturing effort due to air raid damage. It fell to Airspeed Ltd to run the Christchurch Factory, the main aircraft manufactured here being Oxford multi-crew trainers (550 built)

One of many of its type impressed into RAF service, a De Havilland DH-85 Leopard Moth sits quietly on its chocks at Christchurch.

and, later, Horsa gliders (670 built).

Even though not subject to the same heavy and numerous air raids during the period of the Battle of Britain as, say, RAF Tangmere and further east the fighter airfields in Kent, Christchurch did occasionally receive the attentions of the Luftwaffe but casualties and damage on the ground were minimal. Although not a combat unit officially considered as a 'Battle of Britain Squadron', one of the SDF's pilots, Flight Lieutenant Douglas Rayment, shot down an enemy Junkers 88 off the Isle of Wight on 19 September 1940 – only to loose his own life, as did his fellow crewman Sergeant Raymond Sadler, on 17 July 1941 in one of the unit's Blenheim aircraft on a radar calibration flight for TRE Worth Matravers. This work for TRE included trial flying of virtually every airborne radar device which entered RAF service in the early war years, with GEE, Oboe, and Rebecca/Eureka and the first ASV (air to shipping) radars particularly to the forefront.

It was to Christchurch that one of the six KLM DC-3s which escaped from mainland Europe arrived on 13 May 1940, later entering the UK civil register as G-AGGB.

For parts of 1941, a number of Westland Lysander aircraft from No 116 Squadron were based at the airfield, their role being to assist in the calibration of the predictors and radars of guns of the area's Coastal Artillery and anti-aircraft batteries. A lodger unit here from late in November 1941 until the end of hostilities was a detachment from HMS *Raven* at Eastleigh, the function of which was to retrofit specialised electronic kit to aircraft of the Fleet Air Arm.

An incident which has since received popular acclaim occurred on 30 April

Centre of interest: the Bücker Bü 131 Jungmann at Christchurch, still in Luftwaffe markings.

A Blenheim Mk 1F night fighter at Christchurch in late 1940, which was fitted with the latest Mk IV airborne radar which was then being developed there. The crew wait under the port wing whilst the groundcrew investigate an engine defect.

The aircraft in the background is a Douglas A-20 Havoc, one of a batch originally intended for the Armée de l'Air, but diverted to UK after the Germans invaded France. A number were installed with Mk IV airborne intercept radar at Christchurch.

Manpower and machinery: laying the 1944 wire mesh runway. With a length of 4,484 feet (1,366 metres), the runway was rather short for heavily laden P-47 Thunderbolts, the aircraft for which it was primarily laid.

1941 when two former French Armée de l'Air pilots, Dennuy Broudard and Jean Hebert, escaped to England by stealing a German Bücker Bü 131 Jungmann trainer aircraft from Caen and flying it a low level across the Channel to Christchurch. (It later entered RAF service with the serial number of DR626, but when on display in London for 'War Weapons Week' it was so badly damaged by souvenir hunters that it never flew again.) In August, the Anti-Aircraft Co-operation Unit having already been disbanded, the Special Duties Flight moved away to nearby RAF Hurn, at which time Christchurch became a satellite airfield to Hurn and the work at the Airspeed factory generated the majority of the local flying activities.

February 1942 saw the first of the Horsa gliders built at Christchurch depart, towed out by an Armstrong Whitworth Whitley tug, and by the end of the contract another 694 Horsas would have parted in similar fashion, the tugs often being Armstrong Whitworth Albemarles as well as the older Whitleys. As far as work on powered aircraft went, in addition to the building of the Oxfords already mentioned, the factory facilities were also used to fulfil a contract to convert Supermarine Spitfires to Seafires for the Fleet Air Arm, the main obvious external differences being the installation of an arrestor hook and, from the Mk III variant onwards, folding wings. A number of De Havilland Mosquitoes were also assembled at Christchurch, and throughout the war years members of the Air Transport Auxiliary, some of them the most attractive of young ladies, could be seen at the airfield engaged in the ferrying of aircraft to where they were needed for training or operations.

Despite its south coast location, Christchurch had been little used operationally, so it came as no surprise when in March 1944 the USAAF moved in, entitling the base Station # 416. At the same time to the south of the original runways USAAF combat engineers and the British 83rd Engineering Battalion laid down a new wire mesh main runway (24/06), but with a length of just 4,800 ft (1,463 m) this was

15

A slightly out of focus aerial view looking southward across Christchurch airfield. The buildings of the shadow factory are prominent in the foreground, and immediately beyond them can be seen the 'old' runways. The USAAF built runway lies beyond the line of trees. At the top right of the picture can be seen Hengistbury Head, the location of RAF Southbourne.

still 'short' for heavily laden aircraft with a high wing loading, such as the P-47 Republic Thunderbolts of the USAAF's 84th Fighter Wing. Christchurch was not a popular posting with our US cousins, for most of the accommodation was tented and no hangars were provided to allow aircraft maintenance to be carried out protected from the elements. Even though it was a USAAF station, the base was still in the ownership of the RAF, and this practice continues today where, for example, in East Anglia the major USAF bases at Mildenhall and Lakenheath are officially entitled RAF Mildenhall and RAF Lakenheath.

It was, of course, to participate in the softening up of enemy targets in north-west Europe that the Americans came to Christchurch and by and large, for the three months that they were there, things went well and much was achieved against tactical targets such as radar sites, gun emplacements, traffic choke points, headquarters buildings, communications facilities and the like. The USAAF squadrons were the 509th, 510th and 511th Fighter squadrons. Until the forward airstrips were fully operational in the Normandy countryside the P-47s continued to fly from Christchurch, and it was on 29 June 1944 that tragedy struck the local village of Mudeford when a Thunderbolt of the 509th Fighter Squadron failed to gain sufficient height on take-off and crashed into two bungalows in Foxwood Avenue. One of the under-slung bombs exploded on impact, killing the pilot, with the blast bringing down the second aircraft in the combat pair, the pilot of which survived with minor injuries. A total of sixteen people were killed in the initial crash and subsequent explosions, including four members of the British fire crew, 2nd Lieutenant A F Williams Jnr – who was killed as he tried to warn others of the danger of unexploded bombs – a USAAF airfield construction sergeant and a number of unlucky civilians. The bitter irony of this crash was that the squadron was due to leave Christchurch the next day for France.

With the USAAF gone and the RAF making precious little use of Christchurch, the Ministry of Aircraft Production took over Christchurch as a factory airfield on 10 January 1946 and Airspeed expanded its activities. As far back as 1943, and alongside its wartime commitments, Airspeed – by then wholly owned by De Havilland – had started research into what was to become the civilian Ambassador airliner, and which made its maiden flight here on 10 July 1947. Although it had only two engines, its streamlined fuselage, tricycle undercarriage and triple tailfins put many in mind of the much larger Lockheed Constellation, but unlike its American competitor it was not a commercial success and the only customer for the type was British European Airways. Later aircraft built or extensively modified at the factory included the De Havilland Vampire, Venom and Sea Vixen, and for which the wartime runway was replaced by one laid to tarmac.

Aircraft production ceased in 1962, but the airfield soldiered on until 1967 – with the RAF presence being maintained until 1963 by No 662 Volunteer Gliding School (which had been established at Christchurch in 1944 as No 89 Gliding School) before it moved on to Old Sarum and later to Upavon, where it remains today as No 622 Volunteer Gliding Squadron. At the time of leaving Christchurch the school was equipped with Sedbergh T21 and Kirby Cadet Mk III aircraft, both being products of Slingsby Aviation and stabled overnight in a small hangar of

No 622 Volunteer Gliding School in the 1950s, with the Officer Commanding Flight Lieutenant Ron Hayter second from the left – a posed photograph for a visit by the Commandant Air Cadets (centre). The glider is a single seat Kirby Cadet TX Mk 1.

wartime vintage off Mudeford Lane.

With many former airfields, when the runways have been lifted and the hangars demolished, it is often true to say 'today little remains to remind us of the history of the site', but this is far from true at Christchurch. The runway certainly has been lifted and the Air Cadet hangar replaced by a bungalow, but the link with aviation is maintained: the distinctive 'saw tooth roofed' shadow factory building is in active industrial use and many of the streets which cover the former airfield carry aviation names: Andover Way, Brabazon Drive, Britannia Gardens, Dakota Close, Halifax Way, Lysander Close and Vulcan Way, together with the evocatively named The Runway. Additionally, above a plaque bearing the words 'This aircraft is a tribute to the aviation history of Christchurch 1932-62' Sea Vixen XJ580 FAW Mk II stood proudly on a plinth in nearby Somerfield Road from December 1984 until being transferred to Tangmere Aviation, Museum in June 2000, where she remains today.

RAF HAMWORTHY

Although by far the greatest RAF activity in Poole Harbour took place during the Second World War, it is worth noting that No 10 Group had a maritime operational training unit based at Sandbanks from September 1918 to October 1919 and that from 1916 to 1918, initially under RNAS and then RAF control, Short 184 seaplanes flew Channel patrols from Hamworthy.

Civilian flying boat activity was already well underway from the sheltered waters of Poole Harbour when the RAF officially arrived at Poole in June 1942 to establish a new Coastal Command flying boat base to relieve pressure on those at Mount Batten, Devon, and Pembroke Dock on the south coast of Wales. Much of the prime real estate and properties around the harbour had already been commandeered by the other services, so a site for the necessary maintenance slipway had to be chosen to the west of the town at Lake.

Four years earlier Imperial Airways (IAL) (which became the major component of British Overseas Airways Corporation [BOAC] on 1st April 1940) had chosen Poole Harbour as an alternative operating base to its terminal at Hythe on Southampton Water should the threatened war in Europe materialise, the feeling being that the Hythe facility would be especially vulnerable to air attack being so close to the leading civilian port of Southampton and the Naval Dockyard at Portsmouth. Two of the airline's Short S.30 aircraft, G-AFCU and G-AFCV (*Cabot* and *Caribou*), which had an extended range capability, were pressed into RAF service in October 1939, but were both lost near to Bodö in early May 1940 during the early phase of the abortive Norwegian campaign.

Another earlier arrival to the area was *HMS Daedalus II*, established at the Royal Motor Yacht Club premises as a satellite to the main *HMS Daedalus*, Lee-on-the-

Solent, moving in for very similar reasons to those of IAL. Known unofficially as HMS *Tadpole*, because its small seaplanes were dwarfed by BOAC's massive flying boats such as the Boeing 314A *Clippers*, the unit's task was one of basic seaplane training and occasionally providing facilities for covert operations off the coast of occupied France. For substantially more information about HMS *Daedalus II* see the companion volume by Stuart Morris on the Navy: *DORSET, The Royal Navy*.

Preparatory work completed to an initial satisfactory standard, the station became operational on 1 August, and for just the first week of its existence it was known as RAF Poole. This though was not by any means the earliest RAF involvement in the harbour area, for prior to September 1939 trials had been carried out at Poole to assess its suitability for flying boat operations and in the early war years obsolescent flying boats such as twin-engine Supermarine Stranraers and Saro Londons biplanes flew off the waters on an ad hoc basis, with covert operations to France sometimes appearing in their itineraries. Additionally, the RAF's trial Consolidated Catalina Mk I from the Maritime Aircraft Experimental Establishment at Felixstowe paid visits and in June 1940 was involved in a mysterious flight from Estoril in neutral Portugal to Poole carrying senior personnel and priority cargo.

From the beginning of the war there was no civilian flying permitted within the British Isles, save for that authorised by the Air Ministry; RAF Transport Command, from its formation in March 1943, co-ordinated all overseas flights. Thus all of the flying boat operations by BOAC had an element of RAF involvement and, like those by the other international airlines Pan American and American Export, were only permitted to operate within the UK Air Defence Zone with specific permission and the allocation of an IFF (Identification Friend or Foe) code. Throughout the war years there was always an element of cross-operating between the RAF and BOAC, none more so than on the night of 20/21 June 1940 when Captain D. C. T. Bennett (later of RAF Ferry Command, Transport Command and Pathfinder Force fame) flew the Empire Class flying boat G-AFKZ *Cathay* to Biscarosse in the Aquitain region of France to extract Polish General Wladyslaw Sikorski and members of his staff the day before the Government of France signed an armistice with Germany. Sadly Sikorski, the first Prime Minister in Exile of Poland and Commander-in-Chief of the country's formidable armed forces, was killed in an air crash after taking off from Gibraltar in an RAF Liberator aircraft late on the evening of 4 July 1943.

In July 1940, with RAF Coastal Command struggling to operate anywhere near sufficient long range anti-submarine aircraft to meet its widespread commitments, three of the BOAC enlarged Empire G Class aircraft, which had already been modified for military operations, were accepted into RAF service and flown from Dorset by their civilian crews to operate, initially, out of RAF Invergordon on the Cromarty Firth. *Golden Hind*, *Golden Fleece* and *Golden Horn* (carrying RAF serial numbers X8275, X8274 and XX8273 respectively) were used both as anti-submarine aircraft and to ferry priority freight and passengers, often to Gibraltar for onward transit to Malta. *Golden Hind* and *Golden Horn* returned to Poole and

Golden Hind at her mooring in Poole Harbour after resuming wartime BOAC duties.

after refitting to carry 40 passengers in 'austerity' seats resumed BOAC duties in December 1941. (*Golden Fleece* was lost on 21 June 1941 after ditching off Cape Finisterre following a double engine failure whilst en route to Gibraltar.)

On 1 August 1942, No 461 Squadron of the Royal Australian Air Force, which had been formed at Mount Batten from a nucleus of No 10 Squadron RAAF on 25 April, celebrated each year in Australasia as Anzac Day, and hence known always as The Anzac Squadron, became the first operational squadron to be based at RAF Hamworthy, the slipway and technical area at Lake having by then been augmented by a temporary operations room and support facilities alongside Salterns Pier. Many of the groundcrew, and much of the spares and other equipment were brought up from the West Country by rail, the majority in one special train, during August and September and unloaded at Hamworthy Junction – and many of the Australians thereafter always referred to the camp as RAF Hamworthy Junction. The squadron, with 66 operational sorties under its belt at Mount Batten for the loss of two crews, was equipped with Short Sunderland Mk II flying boats and still striving for complete operational effectiveness at the time of its move to Dorset, with a shortage of truly experienced flying boat personnel being one of its problems.

In January of the next year the squadron was able to move its operations room to the first floor of the Harbour Yacht Club and take over part of the nearby Harbour Heights Hotel as an officers' mess, whilst the vast majority of support and domestic accommodation was in requisitioned private houses and the occasional hotel. The flying conditions in the harbour left a lot to be desired. BOAC had had the pick of the trots (as flying boat moorings were known), those left for military use being over three miles away from Salterns Pier and not much nearer to the technical support site at Lake, so both air and ground personnel making their way to and from the aircraft had lengthy boat rides in either direction. Additionally the navigable channels, surrounded by treacherous sandbanks, were very narrow

Two of 461 Squadron's Sunderlands ashore on the slipway at Lake for maintenance.

On the Water. Two of the crew check the Sunderland's nose mooring from the front turret position, which could be wound back, as here, for slipping and picking-up the mooring – a far from easy task in rough sea or strong winds.

for an aircraft as cumbersome on water as a Sunderland and furthermore there were no proper night flying facilities, with aircraft detailed for night patrols often having to fly west to Mount Batten to take-off later to meet their required times on task. (This also affected the squadron later when based at RAF Pembroke Dock, for aircraft from there were towed some 6 miles down to the more spacious Angle Bay for night take-offs.) Despite operating from geographically separated bases, 461's crews as often as not found themselves operating in adjacent patrol areas to their 10 Squadron colleagues and equally often exchanging patrol areas with them at the beginning or end of times on task.

There was one additional pressure on flying boats working out of Poole: The Air Officer Commanding-in-Chief of RAF Coastal Command had a house at Sandbanks looking out over the harbour, and it was not unknown for him to be on the telephone to the Squadron Headquarters when he observed an activity of which he did not fully approve!

The Bay of Biscay was the main area in which 461 Squadron operated, the flying boats' extensive defensive armament – with additional guns carried to those initially fitted to the Sunderlands – helping the crews hold their own in battles with the marauding long range fighters of the Luftwaffe, although one aircraft was lost whilst based at Hamworthy. It is hard to analyse the effectiveness of these patrols, for in anti-submarine warfare the patrolling aircraft could force a U-boat to dive when its crew spotted the aircraft and be deterred from attacking friendly shipping without the aircrew even being aware that they had done so. Job

The wreckage of T9111 before being towed ashore. Note the 'stickleback' ASV radar aerials along the top of the fuselage.

Catalina Mk 1B (PBY-5B) on the Hamworthy slipway. Unlike those on the Sunderland, the Catalina's wing floats are retractable (and form the wing tips when raised).

done! The cavernous interiors of the Sunderlands meant that the aircraft could also act as 'stop gap' freighters and in October they became just that by carrying cargoes down to Gibraltar as part of the build up for Operation Torch.

Early in the New Year, 1943, the aircraft establishment was increased to a dozen aircraft, so the limitations became more of a frustration and soon after the decision was made to replace 461 Squadron and its Sunderlands with No 210 Squadron which was operating the smaller, twin-engined Consolidated PBY Catalina. Thus in April a straight two way swap between RAF Hamworthy and RAF Pembroke Dock was made, but not before Poole Harbour claimed Sunderland T9111 which crashed following an aborted take-off on the 21 March, happily without the loss of any lives. The Bay of Biscay continued to be the focus for the Hamworthy-based aircraft, with six crews from No 119 Squadron normally based at Lough Erne in Northern Ireland despatched to Dorset on one occasion to reinforce 210 Squadron for a specific period of high intensity operations. Amongst the officers who served on 210 Squadron was Flying Officer John Cruickshank who was later to be awarded the Victoria Cross for his bravery in recovering his Catalina to its base in Scotland after being badly wounded by anti-aircraft fire from the surfaced submarine U-347 on 17 July 1944.

As the war continued some improvements were made to the flying facilities in Poole Harbour, but it was still a risky spot to fly from, most especially at night. On occasions in November 1943 flying would also have been difficult for a rather different reason, for during the month RAF Douglas B-20 Bostons and North American B-25 Mitchells carried out extensive smoke-laying trials over the harbour.

23

On 1 January 1944, No 190 Squadron based at Sullom Voe in the Shetland Isles was renumbered as No 210 Squadron and the last of the Catalinas based at Hamworthy were dispersed of, with 'old' No 190 Squadron became an airborne forces squadron. At the same time Coastal Command ceased to consider Poole Harbour as a routine weather diversion airfield, this responsibility passing some thirty miles along the coast to RAF Calshot at the head of Southampton Water, itself a flying boat base since before the Great War.

However, despite the cessation of combat operational flying from the harbour, RAF Transport Command continued to use Hamworthy as the departure base for its Sunderland services to Lisbon (in civilian markings) and India (in RAF colours) although these, and the BOAC services, moved away during spring of 1944 as the build up to Operation Overlord crowded Poole Harbour to such an extent that regular flying operations became impractical until the late summer. RAF Hamworthy was officially closed down on 1 May 1944, but there was to be one final fling here by the RAF when, in September, military Sunderlands once more cleft the waters of the harbour when returning to the UK with repatriated prisoners of war from the Japanese camps in the Far East.

Considering its importance, the harbour received relatively little attention from the Luftwaffe, perhaps the most significant raid being that in June 1942 which saw the destruction of one of the Lake Fuel Depot fuel storage tanks and a major fuel leak. The depot was initially established to meet the needs of IAL, later came under the control of the RAF and – with good connections to the road, railway and, via a small pier, shipping – it eventually met the aviation fuel needs of all the airfields in Dorset and West Hampshire.

The 31 March 1948 saw the BOAC close down at Poole and return to Hythe, where flying ceased on 26th September 1958 with the departure of Aquila Airways' Short Solent flying boat G-ANYI for Madeira, BOAC having ceased maritime air operations on 3 November 1950.

When in 1995 I wrote the book *Military Dorset Today* I concluded the entry on RAF Hamworthy by stating 'sadly there is no plaque anywhere to record the bravery of those who operated from RAF Hamworthy'. This is no longer the case, the Poole Flying Boats Celebration having erected a series of information boards in strategic places around the harbour which, together with the PFBC's active research programme, ensures that the memory of this important site in aviation's history will not be forgotten. Other artefacts still to be seen include the former watch office (control tower) at 68 Lake Drive, now converted to a private residence, the slipways at the former RAF technical area, now part of the Royal Marine's Base, and the remains of the fuel depot on the shore side on Ham Common at Lake.

RAF HURN

Work commenced on the airfield at Hurn, then in the County of Hampshire, in the autumn of 1940 just as the RAF was 'getting its breath back' after the Battle of Britain, and was planned initially as a satellite station to the fighter airfield under construction at RAF Ibsley, near Ringwood, which itself only became operational in February 1941. Located to the north of Bournemouth and Christchurch and bounded by the Rivers Stour and Moors, it was of the standard triangular pattern three runway construction, with the longest surface being 5,200 ft (1,585 m) long. The communal site and living quarters were dispersed to woods around Hurn village. RAF Hurn was declared operational in July 1941, with an early arrival being the Special Duties Flight from RAF Christchurch with its mixed bag of aircraft, which in the main were participating in the radar (both detection and navigation) trials being conducted at Worth Matravers. It was an especially well provided for airfield, with copious hard standings and seventeen hangars, the largest number of which were of the design known as the 'Blister'.

The plan for Hurn to be a fighter airfield were soon changed and just before

Wartime view of RAF Hurn taken by the crew of an aircraft from No 105 (Transport) Operational Training Unit. Note the disruptive markings and imitation hedges, both elements of the scheme to camouflage the site.

An Armstrong Whitworth Whitley of No. 297 Squadron, based at Hurn, standing ready to pick up paratroops at Ringway, Cheshire, for a Combined Operations exercise (IWM 6055).

Christmas 1941 a detachment of Consolidated Liberator B-24 aircraft of No 1425 Flight from RAF Honeybourne, on the Worcestershire and Hereford borders, arrived. The Flight was later to form the core of No 511 Squadron. Its aircraft, however, were not the maritime patrol aircraft in use in the RAF's Coastal Command or the heavy bombers of Bomber Groups of the USAAF, but were unarmed conversions to the transport and communications role and operated a VIP passenger and priority freight service – mainly out to Gibraltar, from whence a further detachment on 'The Rock' maintained a link with the besieged island of Malta.

In the spring of 1942 1425 Flight moved from Hurn to its new base at RAF Lyneham in Wiltshire, some of the trials aircraft were despatched elsewhere and Hurn made ready to receive No 297 Squadron, which arrived in June, and No 296 Squadron which arrived shortly afterwards, with their Whitley aircraft employed in the paratroop-dropping role. In addition to the many parachute dropping exercises in which the squadron crews participated, crews from both squadrons were employed in leaflet dropping over occupied Europe, thus giving them practice of flying in hostile skies. During this same period North American Mustang Mark 1 aircraft of No 170 (Army Co-operation) Squadron were detached to Hurn to fly tactical reconnaissance sorties over Europe.

Towards the end of October 1942 both 296 and 297 Squadrons moved out of Hurn to allow the base to be utilised by the USAAF in operations in support of Operation Torch, the Allied landings on the north coast of Africa from the Atlantic coast of Morocco to as far east as Algiers, which commenced on 8th November. Up to 115 Douglas C-47 Skytrains, 55 transport variants of the B-17 Fortress and a number of B-24 Liberators were the main aircraft involved. By December 296 Squadron had returned to Hurn and shortly afterwards was re-equipped with

The control tower at Hurn in early post-war years, very little changed from its RAF days. The fire engine looks as if it is probably ex-RAF – it carried banks of CO2 rather than foam as an extinguishing agent. The visual control room was also little changed – two controllers at the control desk and their assistant on the telephone.

Armstrong Whitworth Albemarle aircraft, a twin-engined medium bomber which had been found lacking for its design task but excellent for use by the Airborne Forces as a glider tug and, via a floor hatch, the dropping of parachutists. The construction of the Albemarle was unusual: when a shortage of aluminium had been feared, Armstrong Whitworth had come up with an alternative steel and timber construction technique, with little weight penalty. As had the Whitleys been some while previously, the aircraft were utilised for pamphlet dropping over occupied Europe and on occasions, despite the reservations about its performance as a bomber, participated in bombing attacks.

Indicative of the high expectations of the glider force in the operations which lay ahead to invade Europe, No 1 Heavy Glider Maintenance Unit was formed at Hurn in May 1943, initially to prepare Horsa gliders for their long towed flights to airstrips in North Africa prior to participation on Operation Husky, the July 1943 assault landings on the south coast of Sicily – the first stepping stone on the Allies' long hard-fought battle through Italy. Also based at Hurn in support was No 3 Overseas Air Despatch Unit, which arrived there in February and remained until August 1944, thus covering also the Overlord landings and immediate follow up. The flights to North Africa normally began with the gliders being ferried down to RAF Portreath on the north coast of Cornwall and thence the 1,300 mile haul across the Bay of Biscay to Morocco, where interceptions by Junkers Ju 88s and Focke-Wulf Fw 200 Condors were not unknown, followed by a further leg of over 900 miles over the Atlas Mountains to Tunisia. This same summer also saw aircrew from Russia at Hurn converting to, and then departing eastward with, a number of Albemarle bombers which had been gifted to Stalin's Government by the British authorities.

By October 1943 the vast majority of the ferrying requirement had been met. No 296 Squadron had returned from its sojourn in the Middle East, an element of 295 Squadron had joined it at Hurn, later building up to full strength and, in November, No 570 Squadron was formed at Hurn as another Airborne Forces squadron. All three of these units were by now flying the Albemarle and, as well as being heavily involved in training, carried out supply drops to the French Resistance, the Maquis. Then in March 1944 they moved inland to RAF Harwell in Oxfordshire to make way for ground attack Hawker Typhoon aircraft of the Royal Canadian Air Force's 438, 439 and 440 Squadrons carrying out softening-up operations ahead of Operation Overlord, although at that time only a very few 'Bigot-cleared' personnel knew any detail of the proposed landings on the Normandy coast. It was also at this time that No 125 Squadron relocated to Hurn from RAF Valley on Anglesey, a night fighter squadron equipped with the Mark XV1 variant of the De Havilland Mosquito. Later in the spring No 604 (County of Middlesex) Squadron – also Mosquito-equipped – moved down from RAF Church Fenton in Yorkshire to boost Dorset's night fighter defences, both units still managing to make kills in skies now rather starved of significant Luftwaffe activity.

In April three further Typhoon squadrons arrived at Hurn – the RAF's 181, 182 and 247 – and the six squadrons together commenced concentrated operations over northern France, using both free-fall bombs and unguided rockets to complement the awesome firepower of the Typhoon's 20 mm cannon.

All of the Hurn based squadrons were actively involved in Operation Overlord, with the Mosquitoes bringing down ten enemy aircraft in the two nights immediately following the landings, a commendable haul by any standards! The Typhoons were also in the thick of things, with their main targets being enemy

Hawker Typhoon pilots at Hurn in 1944.

armour which, lacking the protection offered by a favourable air situation was especially vulnerable, and radar sites. As the Allied armies moved inland from the beaches airstrips became available for deployment forward of the Typhoons, and by the end of June all six squadrons were operating from the other side of the Channel – leaving room at Hurn for new residents. Save for a short sojourn there by No 418 Squadron of the RCAF with its Mosquitoes VI intruder aircraft, the newcomers did not in fact arrive until 5 August when USAAF B-26 Martin Marauder medium bombers from the 397th Bomber Group moved in from their base at Rivenhall in Essex to carry out attacks behind the German front line on strategic targets such as railway marshalling yards and road and canal chokepoints, with the destruction of bridges being the unit's speciality. The Marauders flew out to a newly constructed airstrip at Gorges in Lower Normandy on 30th August, and once more RAF Hurn was devoid of front line units.

During September the USAAF decided that it no longer needed Hurn as a base and handed it back to RAF Fighter Command, which at midnight on 31 October handed it over to Director General of Civil Aviation. It was soon to become the country's main international airport (until London/Heathrow became operational in 1946), although as early as the spring of 1942 BOAC had been using some of the hangars to the north of the main runway. Avro Lancastrians and Yorks, Lockheed Constellations, and Douglas DC-3s graced the local skies in these early, expanding days of civil aviation – when flying was still an adventure for, mainly, the rich and accidents were rather to be expected.

Former RAF hangars in 1977, then in the hands of the former British Aircraft Corporation. Two BAC-111 jets grace the taxiway immediately south of the hangars.

In the post war years the RAF's involvement at Hurn has been minimal. On 11 December 1978 Southampton University Air Squadron and No 2 Air Experience Flight moved to Hurn from Hamble, Hampshire, the UAS being equipped with the Scottish Aviation Bulldog T1 and the AEF the De Havilland Chipmunk T10 aircraft. In 1988 the UAS moved north to Boscombe Down, on Salisbury Plain, the AEF soldiering on at Bournemouth with its Chipmunks until April 1996 when it received replacement Bulldogs and joined company once more with the UAS. With side-by-side seating, excellent all round visibility and a tricycle undercarriage, the Bulldog was certainly a better aircraft for the task of giving air experience flights to the young members of the Air Cadet organisation. Today both units remain at Boscombe Down – but now equipped with the Grob Tutor T Mk 1 aircraft, which entered service with the RAF in 2001and serves at the fourteen of the UASs and twelve AEFs nationwide.

On the north side of the runway many of the wartime hangars remain, with Cobham Aviation, formerly Flight Refuelling Ltd, amongst the occupants and continuing a connection with the RAF, for the company's Dassault Falcon 20 aircraft – often in co-operation with the BAE Hawk aircraft of No 100 Squadron, based at RAF Leeming in Yorkshire – provide target facilities of a wide variety for British and NATO forces. During the 1950s civilianised Hurn saw many of the aircraft that were later to carry RAF roundels during their flight testing times, with Weybridge-based Vickers-Armstrong establishing a production line and test facility here which saw Valetta transports and Varsity trainers in the local skies, as well as the first of the V-bombers – the Valiant. Sadly the prototype, WB210, was lost on 12 January 1952 following an uncontrollable engine fire, but with all the crew (save the RAF co-pilot, Sqn Ldr Brian Foster, who was fatally injured when his ejector seat hit the tail fin) parachuting to safety.

In January 1991 memories of the wartime years and the airfield's defences were recalled when a bomb disposal unit was called in to make safe 35 pipe mines which were discovered under the runways!

Occasional, but regular, RAF visitors are Lockheed C-130 Hercules and Boeing Chinook helicopters, whilst in the flying display season the aircraft and support

The RAF at Hurn in the 21st century: Lancaster PA474 and Hurricane LF363 of the Battle of Britain Memorial Flight and (bottom) the Red Arrows taxiing in after their display.

personnel of the Battle of Britain Memorial Flight and the Red Arrows Acrobatic Team deploy here to participate in the annual Bournemouth Air Festival and other air shows in the south of England. The bravery and skill of those who pilot the Hawk T1s of the Red Arrows still comes at a cost, as shown by the tragic death of Flight Lieutenant Jon Egging after a display at Bournemouth in August 2011.

Today Hurn is the only former RAF airfield in the county still in active aviation use, now under the name of Bournemouth Airport. The airport serves a respectable number of airlines with scheduled or holiday charter destinations as diverse as

Finland, the Canary Islands, Malta GC, Tunisia, and Cyprus. The old main east/west runway (08/26) has been extended to 7,253 ft (2,211 m) and is used for all large aircraft movements, whilst the short north/south runway (17/35), which had formerly been available for use by light aircraft use when winds conditions demanded it, was taken out of service in soon after the change in ownership. Modern instrument landing systems, with distance measuring equipment (ILS/DME), serving 08/26 allow instrument approaches to these runways in the poorest of weather conditions, and the airport is ideally suited to receive most aircraft short of Boeing 747 and Airbus 340 size on diversion from the main internal termini in the south-east of England. Additionally the National Air Traffic Services College of Air Traffic Control is located at Bournemouth, preparing air traffic controllers and assistants for a career in what is a demanding but rewarding aviation environment. The airfield air traffic control tower, a separate structure completely to the building housing the College, dates back to the RAF wartime years and, heavily modified, continues in use today.

Not directly related to the airfield at Hurn were two local ground units which played their part in the overall war effort: No 12 Recruits Training Centre, until April 1941, and No 3 Personnel Reception Centre, which was operational from July 1941 to January 1946 and was mainly a receiving centre for aircrew from overseas, particularly Australia and Canada, and who were on their way to join their squadron, usually via an Operational Training/Conversion Unit.

Hurn has certainly come on a long way since the first turfs were lifted in 1940 and then, in civil guise, BOAC, Qantas, KLM and Sabena flew the early post-war services from there even before the fighting had ceased in Europe in World War II. With a new terminal building, which opened in June 2010, its future seems assured.

RAF TARRANT RUSHTON

Work, budgeted at £1,000,000 and contracted to the renowned construction company Wimpey, started in May 1942 on the laying down of the last of the RAF's airfields to be built in the county, the site being on an elevated chalkland plain to the east of the River Tarrant and within sight of the earthwork remains of the Iron Age hill fort at Badbury Rings. It was of the standard three concrete runways layout, with four large T2 hangars and some three hundred or so support buildings.

By this stage in the war construction techniques had advanced and in only one year the base was ready for occupation by units of the Airborne Forces of No 38 Wing, but the slow gestation of the glider-towing squadrons meant that operational readiness was not declared until October. The first squadron to form up was No 298, equipped initially with seventeen Halifax Mk 5 aircraft and seven

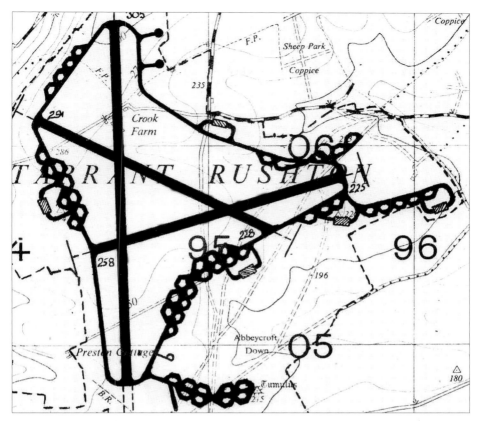

Sketch plan of the airfield as completed. The main north/south runway was 6,000 feet (1,828 metres) long and the subsidiary runways 07/25 and 11/29 were each of 4,200 feet (1,280 metres). Two round and 48 loop hardstandings were provided, together with 11 underground fuel tanks, each with a fuel capacity of 12,000 gallons (54,553 litres).

Tetrarch tank leaving its Hamilcar glider in the summer of 1944, and restored Tetrarch at Bovington Tank Museum today.

33

Looking very sorry for itself. Stirling QS-Q, piloted by Flt Sgt McNamara of 620 Squadron, carried out a wheels up landing at Tarrant Rushton after being hit by flack and loosing a propeller, which severed hydraulic lines, during a 1943 raid on Tours. The bomber has had its engines removed and still perches on the caterpillar trolleys used to pull it clear of the runway.

Horsa troop-carrying gliders and the exceptionally large Hamilcar glider – unique in its ability to carry a light tank. The tank in question was the Vickers-Armstrong Tetrarch, a 3-crew vehicle armed with a two pounder (40 mm) gun and co-axial Besa machine gun, an example of which can still be seen in Dorset today in the Tank Museum at Bovington. The tug aircraft were manned by RAF or Commonwealth air forces personnel, but the glider pilots were all from the Army, although they received RAF aircrew training. In addition to their piloting skills they were trained to a high level as combat troops, thus ensuring that they could make their own positive contribution on the battlefield before repatriation back to the UK.

In February 1944 the Stirling heavy bombers of 190, 196 and 620 Squadrons, by then largely replaced in Bomber Command's Order of Battle by the Lancaster and Halifax, deployed forward to Tarrant Rushton to carry out hazardous low level night supply drops to units of the French resistance, these continuing until well after the D-Day landings.

It is for its involvement in the airborne phase of Operation Overlord that Tarrant Rushton is probably best remembered, and specifically for the part it played in the relief of the very first French village on the morning of D-Day – Bénouville – alongside the bridges over the Caen Canal and the River Orne. Six Halifax aircraft of 298 and 644 Squadrons towed Horsa gliders carrying members of the Oxford and Buckinghamshire Light Infantry (supported by a small number of sappers) under the command of Major John Howard across the Channel for a *coup de main* attack on the bridges, thus preventing German forces from blowing them up, securing them against German counter-attack and keeping them available for Allied forces when the time was ripe for the essential breakout from the Normandy Bridgehead. The landing of his glider less than fifty yards from the barbed wire entanglements around the canal bridge by Staff Sergeant John Wallwork is considered by many to have been no less than the finest flying feat of the Second

Tarrant Rushton on D-Day – 6 June 1944. Horsa and Hamilcar gliders line up on runway 01 with their Halifax tugs, 644 Squadron beyond the runway and 298 Squadron nearer the camera, waiting to taxi into position to have the towline attached. In the distance can be seen the Iron Age hillfort at Badbury Rings, typifying the ancient countryside for which those manning these aircraft were fighting.

World War. This of course was but part of the overall Tarrant Rushton effort for D-Day. Thirty Halifax/Horsa and 3 Halifax/Hamilcar combinations took part in the assault landings (Operations Mallard and Tonga) during the morning of 6 June and 30 Halifax/Horsa and two Halifax/Hamilcar pairs in those just prior to sunset, with in each case the tugs carrying out bombing missions before returning to base. All were part of an airborne force of over 1,200 airborne forces aircraft which flew sorties on D-Day, carrying 20,000 British, Canadian and American troops from three Airborne Divisions across the English Channel. Of these, some 7,000 landed in the drop zones on the eastern flank of the beachhead between the rivers Dives and Orne.

As the battle for Europe continued Tarrant Rushton was in the ideal position to act as an airhead for casualties being flown out from the battlefields, being adjacent to both the US 22nd General Hospital at Blandford Camp and the 106th General Hospital at Kingston Lacy. The speed advantage of the, mainly, Dakota flights which landed here with their wounded over the cross-Channel passage, with lengthy road journeys at either end, must have saved many a life.

The rest of the summer months were taken up in general training, re-supply operations and limited participation in tactical bombing operations, then in September Tarrant Rushton was once more heavily involved in an airborne assault – this time Operation Market Garden, General Montgomery's ill-fated attempt to speed up the advance on Berlin by encirclement of the Ruhr after securing the bridges over the Rivers Waal, Maas and Lower Rhine. On 17 September the

35

Group picture of the aircrew and ground personnel of No 298 Squadron at Tarrant Rushton after re-equipping with radial engined Mark III Halifaxes.

same two squadrons towed across 41 gliders (Hamilcars and Horsas), which initially met little opposition. Sadly the days that followed saw German resistance strengthening and, at Arnhem, it all proved to be 'a bridge too far', the follow-up re-supply missions flown proved to be in vain and by the 25th the battle was lost.

The two squadrons, by now re-equipped with radial engine Hercules-powered Halifax III aircraft, moved out to RAF Woodbridge, in Suffolk, for the last mass glider operation of the war – Operation Varsity, the crossing of the Rhine in March 1945 – and then returned to Tarrant Rushton to carry out SOE support missions in Norway and Denmark prior to landing the 1st Airborne Division at Copenhagen on 8 May, the day after hostilities ceased in Europe. The final major effort from

A Flight Refuelling Ltd Lancastrian over Berlin during the Airlift of 1948/49.

The Meteor being refuelled by a Lancaster with Poole and the Harbour in the background during the record breaking flight of August 1949.

the airfield was its involvement in Operation Doomsday, the transporting of some 7,000 troops and associated supplies to occupy strategic towns and cities in Norway, where there was still a major Nazi presence.

There was little major activity at the airfield after the fall of Germany. Toward the end of 1945 No 190 Squadron moved in to continue heavy glider tug training and the airfield was used for a while as a mail terminal, but by September 1946 all flying had ceased and the airfield was regulated to a 'care and maintenance' status. In December 1947 the Air Ministry declared that Tarrant Rushton was surplus to its requirements and an air of emptiness and desolation prevailed until in June 1948 the civilian company Flight Refuelling Ltd moved its operations from Ford airfield in Sussex to Tarrant Rushton and the airfield echoed once more to the roar of aero engines. This move coincided with the commencement of the Berlin Airlift on 24 June 1948. On 27 July a company Lancaster left the airfield carrying bulk fuel to Berlin's Gatow airfield and until the end of this epic operation in August of the following year Flight Refuelling supplied 90% of the domestic heating oil, motor spirit and diesel oil into the blockaded German capital. The company, using three Lancaster and nine Lancastrian aircraft, was the first civilian company to fly on the airlift and the last to cease operations.

Still on the subject of fuel and on a topic which was to play, and still does play, a major role in Royal Air Force activities as a 'force multiplier', on 7 August 1949 a fuel probe equipped Gloster Meteor F3 took of from Tarrant Rushton and flew in a huge orbit over southern England whilst carrying out ten air-to-air refuellings from

37

RAF Valiant bombers on the ground at Tarrant Rushton in the 1950s, when the Cold War was at its height.

an Avro Lancaster. This record breaking flight, set up primarily to impress the USAF hierarchy, lasted for 12 hours and 3 minutes, with the Lancaster tanker returning just once to base just to refill its own tanks. As it transpired the USAF, having sent two Boeing B-29 Stratofortress bombers and two Republic F-84 Thunderjet fighters to Tarrant Rushton for conversion to Flight Refuelling's new probe and drogue refuelling method, subsequently decided upon the flying boom system, designed by Boeing, as its primary method of air-to-air refuelling. Nevertheless the US Navy and Marine Corps did opt for the British system, considering it as more suited for carrier-borne aircraft operations.

The RAF returned in August 1952 when No 10 Advanced Flying Training School was established at Tarrant Rushton equipped with Gloster Meteor aircraft, namely the F4 and T7 variants. Instruction was given by service flying instructors, but all the administration, maintenance and ground handling was provided by personnel from Flight Refuelling, who gained a reputation for always providing a full flight line at the start of the day's flying programme. Many of the ground personnel were former members of the RAF, and the ethos of disciplined work patterns and dedicated commitment carried over into their civilian lives. The RAF had expanded from its post-war low to meet its obligation to the United Nations force in the Korean War, and it was essentially this which had brought about 10 AFTS's establishment, so after the armistice was signed in July 1953 it was not long before the unit closed, that date being June 1954.

The mid-1950s saw the RAF facing the challenge of ensuring that it's V-Bomber Force, which provided the nation's long range nuclear strike force, was not wiped out in a pre-emptive strike by the Warsaw Pact. The challenge was met in two main ways: dispersal of the Valiant, Victor and Vulcan aircraft to airfields away from their main bases and the ability to scramble (from both main and dispersal bases) within four minutes of a warning of an incoming missile attack being received. Quite extensive works were carried out at Tarrant Rushton, but NATO's deterrent force did in fact deter and thankfully, even in the Cuban Missile Crisis of October 1962, the facility never had to be used in anger.

Despite an income from air-to-air refuelling business and a contract to convert a number of by now obsolescent Meteor aircraft to radio controlled drones for target work, the cost of keeping this large airfield could not be justified and Tarrant Rushton was closed on 30 September 1980 and Flight Refuelling moved to Hurn Airport, where it still has a major presence on the north side of the aerodrome. For a very short while light aircraft and glider flying continued, but in January 1981 work commenced on returning the site to farming and ditches were dug across the runways prior to the major task of lifting the concrete commencing.

Today the atmosphere of a large aerodrome is still present, for even with the runways lifted and many buildings removed this large flat expanse still cries out 'airfield'. On the main site the taxiway and a narrow section of runway 01/19 two are in use as farm tracks and T2 hangars remain standing, together with an aircraft shed and a couple of Nissen huts. Opposite the former camp entrance two buildings from the former communal area remain in use and a little further out to the north east the remains of the operations block can still be seen. Adjacent to the former main entrance to the airfield stands a simple stone plinth, upon which are mounted two memorial plaques. Dedicated in 1982, the top one commemorates all who operated from the airfield during the period 1943 to 1980, from airborne forces to Flight Refuelling, whilst below it is affixed a plaque honouring 'all who served with 298 & 644 Sqns, RAF, and C Sqn, Glider Pilot Regiment'. From 1982 to 2005 annual remembrance services were held at the memorial, although the passage of time has now brought these to an end.

'We will remember them.' A recent Remembrance Day Service at former RAF Tarrant Rushton.

A very early aerial view of RAF Warmwell, with two of the three Bellman hangars to be erected in the south east corner of the airfield already in situ, and with a fair sprinkling – at least 24 - of aircraft of the types used in the station's training role to be seen.

RAF WARMWELL

If ever an RAF airfield could be described as being 'in the right place at the right time' it must, as we shall see, be that at Warmwell, for when the aerial battles of the summer of 1940 erupted the airfield here was right in the front line.

Opened on 1 May 1937 as No 6 Armament Practice Camp to support the shortly to be commissioned bombing and gunnery ranges off the Chesil Beach, the airfield was originally known as RAF Woodsford, the nearest recognised village. It was located where today we see the large and still expanding village of Crossways, but in the late 1930s there was no village there – just a few scattered houses along, mainly, Dick O' The Banks Road – so RAF Crossways was never considered as its name! The original flying field was twice expanded to the west as activity levels increased.

The first Station Flight of aircraft consisted of Avro Tutor and Westland Wallace target tugs and the first squadrons to utilise the training facilities were 206 and 220 of Coastal Command with their Avro Anson aircraft, and as war approached and rearmament proceeded apace, numerous other squadrons came south to Dorset to hone their skills of battle. In January 1938 the training unit was renamed as No 6 Armament Training School, better reflecting its role, whilst in July the name of the station itself was altered to RAF Warmwell to avoid confusion with the Avro

40

Early days at Warmwell: Westland Wallace Mk II during the Armament Practice Camp of 1938 (left) and Boulton Paul P75 Overstrand – both with their operational days well behind them but still suited for training.

Obsolete, but still serving a useful function in the early years of World War Two (with the Fleet Air Arm as well as the RAF) – the Handley Page HP54 Harrow transport aircraft, a conversion of an inter-war years heavy bomber.

factory airfield at Woodford, near Manchester. The airfield site was immediately to the south of the former Moreton airship mooring station, on the opposite side of the Southern Railway's line from Waterloo to Weymouth.

Air-to-air gunnery training was not without risk. Volunteers were sought from the groundcrew to act as winch operators for the target sleeves, and they were paid 6 pence (2½p) per day on top of their basic pay for carrying out these duties.

As it became apparent that 'Peace in our time' after Prime Minister Chamberlain's meeting with Hitler at Munich in October 1938 was not to be, there was a marked increase in activity and almost any aircraft which could be used for gunnery or bombing training appeared at Warmwell, including such obsolescent types as the Handley Page Harrow, Boulton Paul Sidestrand and Fairey Seal. For a short while in the autumn of 1939 Ansons of No 217 Squadron were flown in to fly anti-submarine patrols out in the English Channel, although by the time of the outbreak of hostilities they had moved westward to RAF St Eval in Cornwall.

As the German blitzkrieg rolled across Europe, Fighter Command began to look for airfields to extend its coverage to areas other than the south east of

Looking remarkably cheerful despite their poor accommodation, pilots of 152 Squadron outside one of their bell tents – with canine 'Pilot Officer Pooch' looking on.

the country and, with the major naval base at Portland less than ten miles away Warmwell was an obvious choice, although initially only as a forward operating base for the established fighter base at Middle Wallop on Salisbury Plain. From July 1940 a flight of Spitfire aircraft from No 609 (West Riding) Squadron was always on readiness at Warmwell, being of one third of the unit's aircrew strength and rotating through on every third day. Prior to this 609 Squadron had been based at RAF Northolt, Middlesex, and had been very heavily involved in the fighting at Dunkirk, and even its initial move to the West Country was interrupted by more fighting, for the pilots were instructed to fly direct to Warmwell from Northolt, instead of to Middle Wallop, to act in the defence of the Portland Naval Base which on the 4 and 5 of July was under heavy air attack. The supporting Handley Page Harrow transport aircraft also landed at Warmwell.

There was also a detachment of some thirty of 609's groundcrew permanently at Warmwell under the command of a flight sergeant, with the whole of the detachment being accommodated in tents next to their dispersal, which were well away from the main domestic facilities. Despite the essential – nay, vital – job that these pilots and their supporting groundcrew were doing, the station commander seemed irritated by their presence and intractable over the catering arrangements supposedly provided for them. He wanted to continue running a training unit, not a fighter airfield! The daily flights to and from Middle Wallop were obviously an inefficient way of employing these scarce fighter assets and in July

One man and his 152 Sqn dog, and one man and his 152 Sqn aeroplane: Sgt Edmund Sharp awaits the call to action with his bull terrier Plt Off Pooch as company, and Sgt Bill Kearsey, a Dorset man, poses by his Spitfire Mk 1, R6597.

the resident bombing and gunnery school was despatched northward to Scotland to allow No 152 (Hyderabad) Squadron to deploy south from RAF Acklington in Northumberland with its Mark 1 Spitfires to join 609 Squadron in the fray in the skies over southern England which was to become famous as the Battle of Britain.

Throughout the long hot summer of 1940, Warmwell's Spitfires took off to face overwhelming odds, following the fighter controllers' vectors to intercept Luftwaffe formations as far away as West Sussex and the Severn Estuary, although of course most of the 'trade' was nearer to home and predominately associated with the defence of the docks, oil storage tanks, and barracks at Portland Harbour and around Weymouth. As the contrails high in the blue summer skies above portrayed to those watching from below the fighting was fast and furious but British tenacity, aided by both the strategic and the tactical blunders of Goering and Hitler, saw the aircraft from Warmwell play a significant role in the final victory by 'The Few', the recognised dates of the battle being from 10 July to 31 October, with 18 August being considered the 'Hardest Day' and a turning point in the epic battle, and 15 September 'Battle of Britain Day', the day upon which it became obvious to Hitler that his forces had not broken the back of the RAF in battle and that air superiority for Operation Sealion was not attainable. Sealion was cancelled two days later.

Meanwhile, on 12 August and unknown to those in the cramped cockpits of the fighters above, the valiant battle in the skies was watched from the cliffs of Portland by Prime Minister Winston Churchill, the Commander-in-Chief of the Home Forces, Lieutenant General Alan Brooke, together with Lieutenant General Auchinleck and Major General Montgomery, all of whom were visiting the Dorset and Devon coastlines to assess the readiness of the defences there to resist the anticipated German landings.

Many a pilot struggled back to Warmwell with a battle damaged Spitfire and some escaped with their lives by parachute, but sadly numerous of these brave young men – some barely out of school – fell to their deaths from Dorset skies, and of these some have no known grave. Their final resting places, many of which will be below the waters of the English Channel, are known only to their God.

The flow of combat was not only in one direction, and Warmwell was on the receiving end of attacks by the Luftwaffe, the largest of which during this phase of the war was that on 25 August when seven Junkers 88s, out of a formation of about thirty aircraft, avoided 152's Spitfires and the co-operating Hurricanes of No 17 Squadron from RAF Tangmere and bombed the airfield causing widespread damage but inflicting no serious casualties. On 29 November 609 Squadron redeployed to Warmwell as a whole, but the winter weather saw them involved in little action and they departed for Biggin Hill on 24 February 1941, glad no doubt to say 'goodbye' to their time under canvas in Dorset. The departure was memorable, with the Squadron Leader M. Lister Robinson (who had replaced Squadron Leader H. S. Darley as Commanding Officer in October on his posting to take command of RAF Exeter) leading a full formation of Spitfires across the airfield, with the unit's Miles Magister and de Havilland Puss Moth in the rear, in impressive style. It fell to No 234 Squadron to replace them, their taskings being predominantly in the bomber escort and coastal convoy patrol roles.

By this time, the mass raids of the Blitz period already becoming but a memory, single, probing attacks by low flying fighter-bombers had become the Luftwaffe's main method of carrying the war to England and Warmwell's aircraft were scrambled time and time again to intercept – not always successfully – the intruders. The raiders got through the defences twice in the spring of 1941, on 26 March and 1 April, and in the second attack achieved complete surprise resulting in seven fatalities on the ground, including an off duty pilot from 152 Squadron. The raids continued into the early summer, the last being a heavy and prolonged night attack on 11 May which achieved little in the way of damage.

By the autumn Warmwell's flying and support activities could be divided into two clear categories, in addition to fighters on alert to intercept intruders: our own intruder operations into mainland Europe and activities in support of the newly re-opened Chesil Beach ranges. To add punch to the aircraft carrying out interdictor operations against Fortress Europe, No 402 Squadron of the Royal Canadian Air Force, with its Hurricane IIC 'Hurribombers', was posted in from RAF Digby, Lincolnshire. With a 250 lb (113 kg) bomb slung externally under each wing, four 20 mm cannon and of robust construction, it was an ideal interim aircraft in this role until the more specialised Typhoon came along from the same Hawker stable. 1 November 1941 saw target-towing aircraft based at Warmwell once again.

On 3 March 1942, 402 Squadron left Warmwell to reform at RAF Colerne, Wiltshire, in the fighter role and in its place No 175 Squadron was formed at Warmwell, inheriting 402's aircraft. Early success in the anti-shipping role was

Scenes from No 609 Squadron's days at RAF Warmwell.
Above The quintessential Battle of Britain crewroom scene, as pilots await the scramble bell.
Below Spitfires taxi out for a mass take-off.
Bottom Squadron Leader 'Robbie' Robinson with the Puss Moth 'squadron hack'.

Bombing-up. This Hurricane is an early ground attack variant, for its machine gun armament had not been augmented by 20 mm cannon.

followed by participation in Operation Jubilee, the costly Dieppe raid of 19th August 1942, where – if considered separately from the carnage around the port itself where over half of the six thousand strong landing force were either killed, wounded or taken prisoner – great success was achieved in dive-bombing attacks against adjacent heavy coastal gun batteries.

The following month saw the first of a series of detachments to Warmwell from RAF Exeter by the twin-engined Whirlwind ground attack fighters of No 263 Squadron, which, save for a small number operated by No 25 Squadron at RAF North Weald, Essex, which were later transferred to 263 Squadron, was initially the only unit to fly the aircraft operationally. (Later on a second squadron to operate the Whirlwind was No 137.) Unlike the Luftwaffe which used widely its twin-engined Messerschmitt Bf 110 Destroyer aircraft of similar design, only just 114 Whirlwinds came off the production lines, their major weakness being the unreliable Rolls Royce Peregrine engines and, compared to the single-engined fighters of the day, a lack of manoeuvrability in close combat. Nevertheless, when used as fighter-bomber aircraft they were popular with air and groundcrew alike and achieved good results in sweeps against both shipping and land targets.

As 1942 drew to a close Warmwell was to play an important part in what was to

Hurricane Mark IIE, BE485 AE-W of No. 402 Squadron RCAF, in flight carrying two 250-lb GP bombs. (IWM 4566).

become one of the iconic bomber operations of the war: Operation Chastise, the bouncing bomb attacks on the damns of the Ruhr Valley. The modified Wellington Mk III bomber BJ895 was based at the airfield to participate in a series of scaled down 'Golf Mine' trial bomb drops ('Golf Mine' being the cover name) on the ranges at Chesil, not finally moving away until March 1943. The full story can be read in the entry on the Chesil Beach Bombing Ranges.

Just before Christmas 1943 the 263 Squadron left to convert to the much more capable Hawker Typhoon aircraft – another aircraft which was plagued with power plant problems, this time the Napier Sabre engine, but which were eventually overcome – making the Typhoon one of the aircraft most feared by German armoured forces. Although 263 Squadron had departed for pastures new,

Unsung heroes at work. Groundcrew of No 263 Squadron's 'A' Flight carrying out the daily inspection – the "DI" – on a Whirlwind sheltering in a sandbag revetment in Knighton Wood.

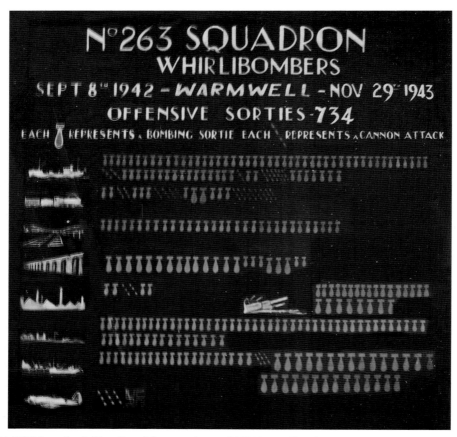

No 263 Squadron's 'Tote Board' from its days at RAF Warmwell, with impressive totals. Shipping: 80 attacks; Trains: 25 attacks; Railroads: 31 attacks; Viaducts: 22 attacks; Factories: 6 attacks; Coastal Gun batteries: 25 attacks; Airfields: 60 attacks; Docks & Harbours: 51 attacks; Aircraft: 3 attacks, including one kill.

Whirlwind P7094 on one of the 'panhandle' dispersals. In the cockpit sits Flying Officer Jim Coyne of the RCAF, the centre of attention on the receipt of his DFC.

Hawker Typhoon – summer 1944. Note the D-Day invasion stripes.

Typhoon 1B aircraft of No 257 Squadron, its pilots having converted to their new steeds the previous September, were often to be seen at Warmwell.

In January 1944, as the emphasis for the Allies turned very much from defence to attack, the USAAF presence at Warmwell became more and more evident, and that of the RAF less and less so, and by early spring the only RAF unit in residence was No 276 Squadron with its Westland Walrus amphibian aircraft dedicated to the Air Sea Rescue role. These obsolescent biplanes, with their single Napier Lion pusher engine, were jokingly referred to as 'Steam Pigeons'!

In March the station was designated as Station 454 of the USAAF's 474th Fighter Group and equipped with the twin-boomed, twin-engined Lockheed P-38 Lightning aircraft, an aircraft not dissimilar in shape to the Whirlwinds of 263 Squadron and employed in a similar fashion as ground attack fighters. Republic P-47 Thunderbolts were regular visitors, often refuelling before and after close escort missions over North West Europe.

As D-Day drew closer so the activity level at Warmwell rose, with the French

Walrus Mark I of No. 275 or 276 Squadron, on the ground at Warmwell (CH 18540).

Ground crew loading a dinghy into a Supermarine Spitfire Mark IIA, P8131 'AQ-C', of No. 276 Squadron RAF at Warmwell, Dorset, during an air/sea rescue exercise (IWM CH 10732).

road and rail transportation system coming under heavy attack in an attempt to ensure that the German Army, the Wehrmacht, would find moving reinforcements to the English Channel coast to try and contain the Allies' breakout from the beachhead extremely difficult. The P-47s flew tactical missions, with the attacks on strategic targets such as marshalling yards being carried out by heavy bombers of both the RAF and USAAF, and with as many, or more, of the sorties being flown in the Pas de Calais region as in Normandy as part of the Operation Fortitude plan to throw the Germans off the scent as to where the actual landings would take place. Meanwhile, as would be expected with the high number of sorties now being flown on operations across the Channel and locally on training flights, 276 Squadron's Walrus amphibians were being kept very busy. In April No 275 Squadron replaced 276 and remained throughout the USAAF period. Its Walruses were augmented by Westland Lysander aircraft, an ideal low level visual search platform which also had the capability of dropping rescue equipment from the light series bomb carriers on the undercarriage spats, and Spitfire Mk VBs, which could get to a search datum a lot faster than either other type and look after itself and, when it got there, keep away German aircraft sniffing around any survivors.

By August 1944 the vast majority of the USAAF aircraft and personnel had left Warmwell to operate from the forward airstrips in France, initially the one at Neuilly, and the emphasis at the base turned once more to armament training, with pilots coming back from the 2nd Tactical Air Force in Europe to Dorset and No 14 Armament Practice Camp to refresh their skills alongside newly trained aircrew waiting to join their first squadrons. After VE-Day the aircrew throughput rate dropped markedly and by the autumn, with VJ-Day also having

The Royal Air Force memorial at Crossways.

passed, the target tugs and their supporting groundcrew had left for the final time, and by November 1945 RAF Warmwell had been officially reduced to a 'Care and Maintenance' status. For a short while parts of the camp were used as a demobilisation centre and as a reception centre for RAF families who had been trapped abroad during the war years, but today the vast majority of the runway areas have been lost to gravel extraction and the domestic and engineering sites have been built on as Crossways rapidly expands. Both of the wartime Bellman hangars remain and the former control tower, with a couple of 'panhandle' dispersals nearby, has been converted into a fine private residence, Egdon House. In West Knighton Woods a few artefacts such as dispersal buildings, revetments and power plinths remain, whilst the finely maintained village hall was a former RAF building used for a wide variety of tasks. In existence for less than ten years, RAF Warmwell certainly earned a commendable place in the fine history of the Royal Air Force.

A memorial, of roughly hewn stone, bearing the Royal Air Force crest and commemorating those of all services and nationalities who made the supreme sacrifice whilst serving at RAF Warmwell, initially RAF Woodsford, was dedicated in June 1989. It is illustrated above and is located near the location of the former operations room, access being gained through iron gates adorned with a pair of Spitfire silhouettes, and it is here each Remembrance Sunday that the parishioners of Crossways gather to remember the fallen.

RAF WINTON

The first airfield in the Bournemouth area with an RAF connection was that located at Ensbury Park, a spot less than two miles to the north of where Bournemouth University now has its main campus, being a replacement flying facility for the earlier and nearby Talbot Village Aerodrome which decamped to the new site following complaints about the noise and general aviation activity in the Talbot Village area. The modern University is built on the Talbot Village airfield site; housing now covers the site of that at Ensbury Park.

Ensbury Park airfield opened early in 1917 and the flying club based there had the distinction of being one of the very few, or possibly the only, civil organisation training pilots for the military during the Great War. Using British Avro 504s, French Caudron G IIIs and American Curtiss JN 3 'Jennies', pilots for the RFC and later the RAF received their basic training here, at what was known to the military as RFC Winton and then, naturally, RAF Winton. For just over a year from 1 April 1918 the RAF's Wireless Telephony School was also based here, moving away to Beaulieu in May of the following year when the RAF presence ceased. Back in civilian use once more, the airfield at Ensbury Park had ceased to be operational by the summer of 1927.

CHICKERELL AIRSTRIP (RAF CHESIL BANK BOMBING RANGE UNIT)

The airfield at Chickerell on the outskirts of Weymouth was not the first in the area, for it was pre-dated by Lodmoor Airfield which was active before the outbreak of The Great War. It was, nevertheless, operational prior to 1 April 1918, for it was originally known as RNAS Chickerell and came under the operational control of the Royal Navy at Portland and with grass runways up to 2,500 feet (762 metres) long and a single hangar. Its original raison d'être was as a landing field for short range anti-submarine aircraft, such as the Airco DH6, operated by No 253 Squadron in co-operation with the airships based at Toller and Upton. The DH6 was designed as a two seat trainer and co-opted for ASW duties in 1917 due to a critical aircraft shortage and was so underpowered that if carrying an anti-submarine bomb it could not also carry a second person to act as an observer. In August 531 Flight of No 241 Squadron replaced 253 Squadron and was there until Armistice Day, leaving Dorset shortly thereafter prior to disbandment in June 1919.

The airfield saw civilian use for a few years, including as the starting point for a short-lived air service to London/Cricklewood Airport, via Bournemouth, and as a venue for air pageants (popularly known as flying circuses). From 1927 up to 1930 the RAF returned on occasions to Chickerell, and then in 1937 the Air Ministry leased the airfield from the local council as a forward operating base for aircraft, mainly from RAF Warmwell, using the Chesil Beach Bombing Ranges. Its main function in its RAF days was to support these ranges and thus its primary use was as somewhere for aircraft to plan to land and refuel and re-arm without having to return to Warmwell. It was also a convenient 'bolt hole' in case of aircraft emergency or unserviceabilities such a jammed guns. However, the short 2,400 ft (731m) grass runway precluded the safe operation of any aircraft larger than a Blenheim or Hampden.

No 613 Squadron Lysander Mk II in the 'Phoney War' days. This aircraft was lost when the crew was forced to bail out over a fog-shrouded Chickerell on 23 April 1940.

As war in Europe came ever more likely, Chickerell's workload increased, with aircraft from the various armament and bombing training units at, mainly, RAF Warmwell landing and departing back to the ranges. These were still the days of the biplane, so aircraft such as the Westland Wallace and its forerunner the Wapiti, the Hawker Audax, the Boulton Paul Overstrand and the Hawker Fury regularly graced the airstrip. If air-to-air gunnery was being assessed, the canvas banner flown behind the target tug aircraft would be examined after the aircraft had landed – the method used being very simple. Each pilot and/or air gunner had his bullet tips colour coded with soft paint, and the number of hits achieved was recorded by simply counting the number of holes in the banner of any particular colour.

In the days of what came to be called The Phoney War, Chickerell continued its main task of supporting activity on the ranges, although the aircraft types changed. Gone were the nostalgic biplanes, to be replaced by tugs such as the Blackburn Roc, Miles Masters and Martinets, and Boulton Paul Defiants, the latter with the four gun turret removed and a winch operator occupying the space behind the pilot.

In April 1940, as hostilities intensified on mainland Europe, a flight of Westland Lysander army co-operation aircraft of No 613 (City of Manchester) Squadron were detached to Chickerell to fly anti-invasion patrols, remaining based in Dorset until mid-May. The Lysander was too slow and carried too small a payload to be of much practical use in its design role, but as an area scout (later to include the search and rescue role) and as a means of ferrying Special Operations Executive personnel in and out of Nazi occupied France it excelled. Amongst those detached to Chickerell was Pilot Officer 'Paddy' Barthropp, who shortly afterwards volunteered for fighter duties and was to become a leading Spitfire pilot during the Battle of Britain, flying with No 602 (City of Glasgow) Squadron out of RAF

Westhampnett (now known as Chichester [Goodwood] Airport). He was awarded the Distinguished Flying Cross for his bravery in combat and until his death in 2008 was Life President of the 613 Squadron Association.

After Operation Dynamo and the evacuation from Dunkirk in 1940 the airstrip was blocked off with old cars and the like, presumably on the assumption that this cleared area very near to the strategic naval base at Portland would have made the ideal drop zone for airborne forces seeking to neutralise the port, but as the battle for supremacy of the skies turned in the RAF's favour and the risk of invasion reduced, the landing area was cleared once more and flying resumed. Spitfires of No 182 Squadron sometimes used Chickerell as a Forward Operating Base and by October it was 'business as usual' when the ranges reopened and for the rest of the war years the base continued to operate in this role. Amongst those based at Chickerell – officially 'Royal Air Force Chesil Beach Range Unit' – were the personnel running the ranges and, towards the end of the war, the personnel of Weymouth's No 40 Air Sea Rescue Unit.

Flying at Chickerell reduced to the occasional visitor level after November 1945 when RAF Warmwell closed down, its resident Armament Practice Camps having departed the previous month, but the base continued to operate as the headquarters for the operation of the ranges. From about 1947 onwards the Royal Navy was making greater use of the flying facilities than was the Royal Air Force, its confined area making it ideal for use by the helicopters by then entering Fleet Air Arm service, the first of these being the Sikorsky R-4B Hoverfly, which had made its initial flight in 1944. This single-seat aircraft had a very limited payload capability, a maximum speed of 75 knots and no attack capability, but it nevertheless led the way to future rotary wing flying in the RN and the trial flying at Chickerell by the Rotary Wing Flight of No 771 Squadron, including the very first landing of a helicopter on a moving warship, was seminal in the evolution of the helicopter as a vital component in any naval commander's inventory. As the 1950s progressed the Hoverfly was displaced by the Westland Dragonfly and then the Westland Whirlwind, both of these aircraft being licence built versions of the Sikorsky S-51 and S-55 respectively and constructed just across the county boundary at Yeovil in Somerset.

By the late summer of 1955 the last of these naval helicopter trials at an RAF airstrip came to a close and there was only the very occasional airborne visitor to Chickerell thereafter – and still only rarely from the RAF. Auster AOP aircraft of the Army Flying Corps were probably the most often seen, sometimes in association with the Territorial Army's use of Chickerell for parachute jumping from a tethered barrage balloon with a wicker suspended below. The training of the paratroops was conducted by RAF instructors and control of the balloon was in the hands of an RAF balloon unit. In 1955 Weymouth's No 1606 Squadron of the Air Training Corps moved into a new hut built on the site just inside the main entrance. In the late 1950s a party of USAF personnel involved in the planning of the Troposcatter

Station at Ringstead were accommodated in Chickerell's wooden huts – a far cry, I suspect, from that which they were more used to, but they were welcome in the local area, where folk still had fond memories of American troops based in the area prior to D-Day. They even got used to warm Devenish's bitter, one of their officers' favourite drinking establishment being the Cutter Hotel in Weymouth town centre.

The last noteworthy use of the airstrip was in April 1959 when helicopters of No 815 Squadron of the Fleet Air Arm used Chickerell in conjunction with a flypast on the 29th when Queen Elizabeth and a young Prince Charles paid a visit to the carrier HMS *Eagle* moored in Weymouth Bay.

In September 1959 a signal was received from HQ Bomber Command advising that the unit would be reduced to a Care and Maintenance and on the 23 October the RAF ensign was lowered for the last time. Today the whole site is covered by housing and light industrial units and there are but a very few reminders of its existence: a small patch of concrete where the camp entrance once was and two streets with names associated with the aviation – Cobham Drive and Stainforth Close.

WORTH MATRAVERS AIRSTRIP (RAF WORTH MATRAVERS)

The airstrip at Worth Matravers was sited inland from St Aldhelm's Head on the western side of the track leading down to the CHL experimental site, below the spot where the National Coastwatch Institution lookout and the radar memorial are sited, and opened early in 1940 to meet the needs of the scientific community based on the headland between Renscombe Farm and the cliff top. It was in essence a satellite airstrip to the airfield at Christchurch.

On the headland there was originally a private aerodrome, which had been opened on 16 August 1928 and operated by the very active Isle of Purbeck Light Aeroplane Club. The club used a wooden construction Simmonds Spartan training/touring aircraft and in 1928 had a total of 128 members (pilots, observers and associates), but was closed before the outbreak of war.

The main activity at the military airstrip was associated with radar trials and the necessity of establishing how effective the new radars would be in detecting non-metallic aircraft, most especially gliders which could have been employed in an assault landing by the Nazi forces on British soil. To achieve the most from the trails the boffins wanted the gliders to depart from the airstrip as well as land back at it, so for the period in question – the early summer of 1940 – up to three gliders on the books of the Special Duty Flight at Christchurch would be towed in their trailers down from Christchurch and rigged for flight at Worth Matravers, after which the required number of Avro 504N glider tugs would fly in ready for the trials. The high performance gliders, some of the most modern in the country at the time and including a German Minimoa sailplane, would then be towed off

High level view of Worth Matravers airstrip and surrounding area, taken in 1940.

seawards to a range of about 40 miles (64 km) and up to about 10,000 feet (3,048 metres) and released. Totally at the mercy of any marauding German fighters over the Channel, the pilots would commence their lonely glides back to the Dorset coastline with, on one occasion at least, the 'wave lift' on the 335 feet (102 metres) cliff face being necessary to make it back to safety after the scientists requested a lower than usual approach path.

These experiments, and a small number where the approach to the headland was made from a landward direction, were concluded by August and the tugs and gliders dispersed of, but not back to Christchurch but to the Central Landing Establishment at RAF Ringway, now the site of Manchester International Airport, and thereafter the strip was just used on an irregular basis by communications aircraft. Sadly, on 14 September 1940, a Miles Magister training aircraft from No 32 Maintenance Unit at RAF St Athan in South Wales which was collecting drawings to take back to 32 MU, crashed on landing with both on board being killed. The uplift from the cliff face which had been so valuable to the odd glider pilot proved fatal to Flying Officer Hinks and his passenger.

The airstrip was finally closed in 1941.

FOUR

THE ELECTRONIC WAR

Although the vast areas covered by the airfields in the county ensured that even today they remain the most obvious symbols of the RAF's presence, located within Dorset were a number of other RAF facilities which played a major part in the Service's contribution to command of the skies. It is worthy of note that during the years of the Second World War there was nowhere in the whole of the British Isles with a higher density of ground-based navigation aids and radars than Dorset.

No story can be written on the RAF's use of radar and other electronic aids without making mention of the Telecommunications Research Establishment (initially the Air Ministry Research Establishment) at Worth Matravers and adjacent St Aldhelm's Head, for although it was not an RAF establishment in itself the scientists working there had a very close relationship with the Service. From May 1940 until May 1942 research and development was carried out at TRE which lead directly to virtually all of the advances in radar technology which were to prove seminal in the winning of the war, and it can be argued that the results achieved here rank in importance alongside the achievement of the breaking of the German Enigma codes at Bletchley Park.

Certainly without the Chain Home radars and the RAF's associated control and reporting system the outcome of the Battle of Britain would have been very different, and without the provision of centimetric air to surface vessel radars for the aircraft of Coastal Command the winning of the Battle of the Atlantic would have been inestimably more difficult and prolonged.

RADARS

Chain Home (CH) radar's basic ability was to detect an aircraft flying at 10,000 feet (3,050 metres) at a distance of 50 miles (80 km). Chain Home Low (CHL) was introduced to allow aircraft flying as low as 500 feet (152 metres) out to a distance of 25 miles (40 km) to be detected, later improved upon even further as microwave radars were introduced.

RAF Worth Matravers

The first of the RAF's new radars in the 'West Coast Programme' for Fighter Command to be completed was that on land at Renscombe Farm, two 240 feet (73 metre) wooden towers having been erected prior to the arrival in the area of

Worth Matravers. View of A, B and E sites at TRE, with part of the airstrip visible in the bottom right hand corner.

'A' site on the headland at Worth Matravers, with the Chain Home radar towers prominent. The Renscombe Farm buildings are very obvious in the foreground, whilst the chalk cliffs above Chapman's Pool fill the middle distance.

21st century remains of the 1940 Worth Matravers Chain Home Low radar site. A replacement was later built higher up on the cliff face, where the National Coastwatch lookout is sited today.

the first of the 'boffins'. Up to that time the westernmost Chain Home radar in the chain around the south and east of England was at Ventnor in the Isle of Wight. TRE began to erect its own aerials in the advancement of its researches, and also rapidly completed a basic CH station using two of the 240 towers, which it handed over to the RAF.

A mobile site was also positioned at nearby Kingston Woods, later being used at RAF Southbourne. When Southbourne became fully operational, the RAF CH facility at Worth was closed down. As well as the Chain Home radar, the headland boasted Chain Home Low and Coast Watch radars. Although nothing remains today at the site of the earliest towers, there are extensive remains to be seen at the headland below the National Coastwatch lookout of the CHL facility.

Radar Memorial at St Aldhelm's Head, unveiled in October 2001.

RAF Southbourne

Located on Hengistbury Head on the north shore of the approach from the west to the strategically important Solent and the important naval base at Portsmouth, the isthmus was occupied by the Army early on in the Second World War, who were joined later by an RAF unit from No 75 Signals Wing from No 60 Signals Group which established RAF Southbourne, a Chain Home radar station, operational from 8 April 1942 until September 1945. The apparatus at Hengistbury Head included some of the kit that was originally allotted to the mobile station for Worth Matravers at Kingston Wood. There was also a Watcher/Monitor and direction finding station located here.

At the radar site were 4 transmitting towers and 2 for receiving (MB1 transmitters; RF4 receivers), together with a number of semi-underground plotting rooms. The domestic accommodation was located in woodland some little distance from the operational site, with a manning level of some 30 personnel.

The whole headland is now a nature reserve and little remains to be seen from the days of military occupation.

Aerial view of the site at RAF Southbourne, probably shortly after it ceased to be operational. Three of the radar towers are clearly visible in the foreground, whilst beyond can be seen Christchurch Harbour and Mudeford.

RAF Ringstead

RAF Ringstead, like Southbourne, was one of the westwards additions to the country's radar chain which entered service after the Battle of Britain had been won. Work commenced just in from the coast at Ringstead Bay in January 1941, with the station declared operational in May 1942 with CH radar. It was originally planned that the operational buildings would be unhardened and a reserve station built nearby, but the local topography precluded this and they were later protected by overhead and side earthworks. The domestic and support accommodation for the unit was located to the north of the radars at Upton.

Ringstead was amongst the stations upgraded from 1949 onwards as Cold War tension rose and continued in service until 1956, closing down when the Rotor radar on Portland became operational. From December 1963 the USAF operated a Tropospheric Scatter facility (officially RAF Ringstead) immediately to the west of the former radar station, its task being to use the various tropospheric layers to bounce UHF radio signals over great ranges with the minimum of atmospheric interference. Advances in satellite technology made the facility redundant and it closed down in 1974.

Radars on Portland

A radar at West Cliff, on Priory Corner, became operational as a triple service use radar station using Army Coastal Defence (CD)/CHL radar in February 1942, but was taken over by the RAF as RAF Westcliffe as a CHL base in August 1942 and remained in service until 1947 with AMES Type 2 CHL apparatus. Drivers negotiating Priory Corner can still see the railings on the steps leading up to where the radar was sited, whilst at the top of these steps those on foot can spot the remains of the buildings associated with the unit.

The Army CD/CHL M72 radar at a site known as East Cliffe, to the south of the Young Offenders Institute, was also taken over by the RAF in April 1942 as RAF Eastcliff, but was considered to be redundant and closed down immediately upon transfer.

RAF The Verne was located within the grounds of the Verne Citadel and was an Air and Surface Watching station operating Types 41, 54 and 57 centimetric radars, the highest of the associated steel towers being 200 feet (61 metres) tall and from which useful radar returns could be obtained from as far away as the French coast. Personnel from The Verne had servicing responsibility for the Eastcliff and Westcliffe radars, even in their Army days. The unit remained operational, with the Type 54 radar only, until the mid-1950s, by which time the Verne Citadel had become a prison, and probably closed down at about the same time as RAF Ringstead, also in the interim having been upgraded.

During the war years, and for varying lengths of time, a number of mobile radar units were also sited on Portland.

The final RAF radar on the Isle of Portland was by far the most impressive, and

The main radar tower at RAF The Verne, seen from the ramparts of the Citadel.

the only one to use the title RAF Portland. With the hardening of attitudes on both sides in the first decade of the Cold War the acceptance that above ground radar buildings, even if hardened, were extremely vulnerable to precision nuclear weapons – and acceptance that current radars were very dated in electronic performance – led to the decision being taken to upgrade the UK's air defence radars, initially by upgrading the wartime CHL stations (such as Ringstead and The Verne). Manned by No 815 Signals Unit, the new radar on Portland was one of eight next generation Rotor R1 radars built, of which the seven others were built underground whilst Portland's was buried in the defensive ditch of the Verne Citadel and then covered over. Save for the radar head itself, all the surface buildings were designed to look 'non-military', the entrance building looking like a civilian bungalow. Access to the operations room was via a lift, the only one of the eight so equipped, with an emergency escape door in the cliff side above East Wears.

The station was handed over to the RAF by Marconi Systems Ltd on 20 February 1953, with the radar itself being upgraded in 1955. It was later planned to install a Type 80 'Green Garlic' radar, but the advances which this radar brought with it made numerous Rotor stations redundant, one of which was Portland's – and which was therefore declared surplus to requirements and ceased to be operational in the autumn of 1959.

GEE

GEE was a hyperbolic navigation system evolved in the early years of the Second World War to meet the RAF's needs at a time when both Bomber, and to a lesser extent, Coastal Commands faced serious navigational problems. Navigation techniques at this time had evolved little from those in use since the Service's earliest days and the requirement to fly tactically by day and by night under conditions of radio and radar silence and often in poor weather called for a position fixing aid which could be operated quickly and simply. Navigation to an accuracy that only resulted in one in five crews dropping their bombs within five miles of their intended targets, as revealed in the Butt Report of 1941, was just not good enough and the introduction into service of GEE was intended to dramatically reduce these miss distances.

The principle of operation was that of measuring the time difference between the reception in the aircraft of pulses from ground transmitters, which were electronically tied to each other, with the time difference between the signals being received being measured on a cathode ray tube display at the navigator's position in the aircraft. The time difference between signals were displayed as peaks on a time base, these readings being used to refer to pre-computed lines on a special chart and from which the aircraft's position could be established. To obtain a position fix, the aircraft had to be within reception range of three stations; a simple position line could be obtained if only within range of two stations.

Navigator's GEE display. (Note the two timebases.)   GEE tower at Worth Matravers.

At short range from the transmitters fix accuracy could be as good as 165 yds (151 m), with accuracy at extreme range of about 400 miles being in the order of two miles. As the system required no transmission from the aircraft it had the major advantage over, for example, airborne radars such as H2S in that when in use it would not give the receiving aircraft's position away. The system was however vulnerable to jamming over enemy territory, but this jamming did not extend back over the British Isles and thus allowed aircrews to navigate by GEE towards their bases at the end of tiring combat sorties.

GEE became operational in March 1942, at the time when Bomber Command was launching the first of the 'thousand bomber raids' and Coastal Command was heavily engaged in its campaign against the German U-Boats in the Bay of Biscay and Eastern Atlantic. A timely piece of equipment!

There were four GEE chains established over the UK: the Southern, South Western, Northern and Eastern Chains. A development by the Americans later in the war of the British GEE was Loran A, which operated on a similar principle but over much greater ranges, with much of the training for the operators for both systems being carried out at Worth Matravers. GEE remained in service until the late 1971; Loran C continues in use in the Americas, but now exclusively as a maritime fixing aid.

Dorset's GEE Stations

RAF Brandy Bay, located on Gad Cliff to the west of St Aldhelm's Head, was a monitor for the Southern Gee Chain, with a reserve transmitting station located alongside it. It had the misfortune of being within the area assigned to the US Army's Tyneham Combat Training Area, operational from December 1943, and the monitor task was passed along the coast to RAF Worth Matravers some time during 1944.

RAF Bulbarrow Hill, which became operational in 1942, was the master station for the Southern Chain, with its slave stations at Thurleigh Hill in Sussex and West Prawle in Devon.

The RAF unit here closed down on 1 December 1957, but the United States Air Force later maintained a facility on the site as part of the communications link between the USAF's 2180 Communication Squadron's Troposcatter Scatter station at Ringstead and the USAF's major communications centre at RAF Croughton, 8 miles south-east of Banbury. This Oxfordshire base still operates today as the home of the 501st Combat Support Wing. An MOD microwave communications tower still stands at Bulbarrow.

RAF Worth Matravers was the 'B' slave station for the South Western Chain, the master of which was at Sharpitor on Dartmoor, and also acted as the monitor station for the Southern Chain on taking over this task from Brandy Bay. In an attempt to throw the Germans off the scent of GEE, Worth Matravers also radiated a 'J' beam, a radio track beam similar in nature to Knickebein radio navigation beams

Worth Matravers GEE equipment and monitoring office.

used by the Luftwaffe, which the enemy detected and for a while considered it, and not GEE, to be a new RAF navigation aid.

Uniformed personnel of the RAF were last based here in 1958, but a civilian party continued to work at the base until 1963. A further RAF unit in Dorset was based within the confines of RAF Worth Matravers in August 1942 – RAF Renscombe Down, an establishment mainly involved in the training of complete crews of operators and support personnel for overseas service with mobile radar and navigation aid detachments. By November that year there were 150 staff and 345 trainees on the unit's strength.

Oboe

Declared operational in December 1942, Oboe was a 'blind bombing' navigation aid designed to indicate to an aircraft precisely at what point to drop its war load, be it target markers or bombs, and was based on transponder technology, which involved the Oboe equipped aircraft re-radiating an electronic signal back to the ground installation whereby its distance from the station could be computed. Some of the experimental CHLs on the TRE site were converted to Mk I Oboe stations.

The Oboe ground stations operated in pairs and sent out radio signals to define a circle of specific radius, which the aircraft's Oboe equipment received and re-transmitted. The ground stations monitored the aircraft's progress towards the target, this – adjusted for altitude, aircraft groundspeed and wind velocity – being the point where the two radiated signals crossed. One of the ground stations, the

The Oboe control room at RAF Tilly Whim, just west of Swanage.

'Cat', guided the aircraft along the required circular track by transmitting signals advising of deviations port or starboard of track, whilst the second, the 'Mouse', measured the aircraft's groundspeed and signalled when the bomb release should be activated. Each station could act in either capacity.

The initial system, which had a range of about 300 miles, had the disadvantage of only being able to control one aircraft at a time, but this shortfall was more than offset by the accuracy achieved. Because of the capacity limitation Oboe was mainly used by aircraft of the Pathfinder Force, often Mosquitoes, which specialised in marking targets for attack by the main bomber stream. A later development, operating at a much higher frequency, was the confusingly named GEE-H, for it was more similar to Oboe than to GEE. Having a capacity of about 80 aircraft at any one time, it went a long way to overcoming the 'number of users' limitation in that transponder was fitted at the ground station.

Dorset's Oboe station, operational from March 1944, was designated as RAF Tilly Whim and worked in conjunction with one or other of the Oboe stations at Beachy Head, Sussex, and Hawkshill Down in Kent. As the battle for Europe moved away from the Normandy Beachheads and towards Germany, it reached beyond the range of the UK fixed Oboe stations, so mobile GEE and Oboe units joined them to enable target designation to continue as far east in Europe as necessary.

RAF Tilly Whim was reduced to a care and maintenance status in February 1945, and today a small display of pictures of the station in its operational days can be seen at Durlston Country Park, which lies a mile out of Swanage and encompasses the former RAF Tilly Whim site.

Mandrel

Towards the end of 1941 the Air Ministry began a programme to jam German early warning radars deployed along the French coast, and from this work the Mandrel jamming system was developed, with four prototype ground stations being constructed on the south coast. Six transmitters were installed at each site producing a jamming barrage over the entire 118 – 128 MHz band used by German radars. New improved consoles were installed in May 1942.

The small RAF unit at Kimmeridge during the Second World War was the westernmost of four stations fitted with Mandrel jamming apparatus and thereby played an important role in combating the effectiveness of the German Freya and Würsburg radars located on the north coast of France, which sought out radar returns from aircraft departing the English coast for continental Europe. Mandrel was also fitted to certain Allied bomber aircraft flying in the main bomber stream to and from a target and sought to achieve similar results. It is in this capacity that it is more normally remembered.

Diathermy Machines

Indicative of some of the emergency measures forced upon the nation during the summer of 1940 was the use of some twelve or so Diathermy machines – clinical instruments for local heating of body tissues for medical purposes which were requisitioned from hospitals – as ad hoc electronic jammers, with the only one recorded in Dorset being positioned at Wimborne Minster Police Station.

1940s Diathermy Machine.

Ping Pong

Established just prior to D-Day, Ping Pong was an extremely accurate ground-based direction finding and radar signal analysis facility, used to 'fingerprint' every enemy radar within range and thus allowing them to be attacked and disabled immediately prior to Overlord. As part of the Allies' deception plan – Operation Fortitude – some radars were deliberately left undamaged in order to mask the location of the planned landing sites and also to enable false information ('disinformation') to be fed to the German forces. Dorset's only Ping Pong site was above the hamlet of Acton, in the Purbeck hills close to Langton Matravers.

Aspirin

The Aspirin jammer was a transmitting devise included as one of the measures taken to disrupt the German X-Beam (Knickebein) transmitter located on the Cherbourg Peninsular. Aspirin wasn't designed, as mythology would tell us, to 'bend' the beam but was a high power transmitter sending out a signal the same as that of the enemy in the hope of confusing the German aircrew. During the winter of 1940/1941 one such device was sited at RAF Southbourne.

RADIO DIRECTION FINDING FACILITIES

In addition to the direction finding apparatus positioned at the county's airfields to assist aircraft to land through cloud, there were three additional sites used by the RAF in Dorset. These facilities belonged to No 80 Signals Wing and reported to their Wing Headquarters at Hatfield in Hertfordshire for intelligence gathering purposes. Located at Hengistbury Head (two) and Parkstone, they were known as Watcher, Monitor or simply D/F stations depending upon their exact function.

Godlingston Hill

Godlingston Hill, with its distinctive Nine Barrow Down summit, lies between the Corfe Castle to Swanage Road and Poole Harbour and was officially a Royal Navy facility. Work on the site, including the introduction of mains electricity to the valley below for the first time, commenced in 1936 and consisted in the main of four underground bunkers, three on the ridge line and a single one at the foot of the hill near Knitson Farm, where the domestic accommodation was located. The facility was a major communications centre for both the interception of enemy shipping and aircraft transmissions and for the broadcasting of 'spoof' information designed to add even more confusion to the fog of war for the Kriegsmarine and the Luftwaffe. So important was the base to the overall Allied effort around D-Day that its guard was bolstered in case the enemy should try and land saboteurs to disrupt its operation, which included the establishment of a sensitive and highly secure communications link to kick into use as soon as the associated equipment was set up on the far shore.

The facility was tri-service in operation. The RAF had J Watch personnel based there whose primary task was to monitor and record all enemy jamming transmissions over the wide frequency band of 20 MHz to 3,000 MHz and attempt to pinpoint the physical source of the jamming, thus enabling ground attack aircraft to be targeted against the jamming transmitters.

As the Battle for Europe moved inland away from the Normandy beaches so the facility's effectiveness at these greater ranges diminished and by early 1945 it had been reduced to a care and maintenance status. Today the bunkers still exist, with the one at lower level and two above abandoned, but with the fourth one still in use for government and local radio communications.

FIVE

BOMBING AND GUNNERY RANGES

CHESIL BANK

As the clouds of war built up over Europe in the mid-1930s, the Air Ministry embarked upon a search for a series of bombing and gunnery ranges in coastal waters around our shoreline. In 1935 it sought nine such ranges, but was only about to identify six sites as being both suitable and available – one of which was in Lyme Bay (also known as West Bay) off the world famous geological phenomena the Chesil Beach, now part of the Dorset and East Devon World Heritage Jurassic Coastline. The area was already in use by the Royal Navy as a training area, with an emphasis on anti-submarine and anti-mine warfare training, and the Admiralty was very reluctant to cede control of the waters to the RAF. Additionally, objections were also raised by local fishermen and naturalists who raised fears, respectively, about damage to fish stocks and to the rare *Zostera Nana* underwater weed which was a major component of the diet of the nearby and internationally famous mute swan colony. On the political front objections were raised in the House of Lords and at a more humble level by both Portland

A group photograph, taken at RAF Warmwell, with a Boulton Paul Defiant target tug aircraft as the backdrop. Having taken a terrible mauling as a fighter, the aircraft was relegated to target towing duties with the winch operator occupying the area where the four gun hydraulic turret was formerly sited, and was a 'regular' off Chesil Beach.

Despite its poor quality, this is one of the most historic photographs taken in Dorset. Wellington bomber BJ895 drops a trial bouncing bomb over the Fleet, with Chesil Beach and Lyme Bay beyond clearly visible. In March 1943 the Lancasters of 617 Squadron were to drop the final version of the bouncing bomb on the dams in the Ruhr Valley, in what is now called the Dambusters Raid.

Urban District Council and Chickerell Parish Council, but all to no avail, and on 1 September 1937 the ranges were declared open.

Initially the fixed targets were of two types: three large moored buoys laid about a mile offshore for bombing practice (using light series practice bombs) which were painted bright red and fitted with a flashing light for night attacks. Additionally, hessian targets were laid on the landward side of the beach for air-to-ground gunnery practice. The range was used for air-to-air firing for both pilots (fixed guns) and air gunners (flexible mountings), with target towing aircraft pulling sleeve targets upon which hits could be recorded. The ranges were controlled by VHF radio and flag signals from the quadrant huts, personnel in these huts also observing 'fall of shot' for aircraft bombing the moored targets. The former Weymouth Aerodrome at nearby Chickerell, now back under the control of the Air Ministry, acted as headquarters for the airmen manning the range.

Without a doubt the most famous use of the ranges was by Barnes Wallis's team developing the bouncing bomb, initially to be used in its final 'Upkeep' form for the raids in May 1943 by No 617 Squadron on the dams in the Ruhr Valley in Operation Chastise. The Dorset range was not chosen just for the suitability of the area for the trials but also because of its secure environment and the fact that bomb drop accuracy assessment apparatus and experience personnel were already in position.

The drops were all from the modified Wellington bomber BJ895, with the first trial carried out on 4th December 1942 – and which was unsuccessful. Apart from the first flight which took off from the Vickers airfield at Weybridge, the aircraft operated out of RAF Warmwell and was normally piloted by Captain J. 'Mutt'

Summers (the test pilot who flew the very first flight in the Spitfire prototype in March 1936) and with Barnes Wallis as bomb aimer. It was not until 23 January 1943 that a successful drop was made, after which the project proceeded successfully to its conclusion. The last drop at Chesil was on 8 March and, unlike the earlier flights where the bomb was dropped on the shallow stretch of water between the beach and the mainland known as The Fleet or Littlesea, this one was conducted in the open sea off the beach. The trials, with full size bombs in modified Lancaster aircraft were concluded at Reculver in Kent.

The departure of the Barnes Wallis trials team didn't mean that the workload dropped – far from it, for in the spring of 1943 a second Fleet Air Arm target-towing unit deployed to RAF Warmwell to use the ranges, honouring an agreement with the Royal Navy made when the ranges were established that its aircraft could use what was essentially an RAF facility. As new aircraft entered the RAF's inventory so they came to Dorset to carry out trials of their defensive and offensive weapons systems, with the oft overlooked maritime patrol aircraft of Coastal Command being as regular users as the better known aircraft of Fighter and Bomber Commands. Naturally things occasionally went amiss, such as the day that a Typhoon pilot managed to put his rockets through the walls of a cottage and the occasion when a Me 109, seeking a target of opportunity, strafed one of the moored targets.

In 1949, with the Cold War now very much a fact of life, the facilities provided were:

1. Three practice bombing targets (wooden, painted yellow and with pole and basket identifiers), and on which only small smoke ('puff') bombs could be dropped.

2. One live rocket projectile firing range, for use only during daylight hours.

3. One combined air-to-ground gunnery (maximum calibre 20 mm) and inert rocket projectile firing range.

In addition to these visual, sometimes bomb or gun site supported, targets, electronic assessments were carried out of practice bombing attacks using the Gee navigation aid.

In January 1951 No 217 Signals Unit, a mobile radar unit, was formed at RAF Bawtry, near Doncaster, and moved to Dorset to exercise radar control of aircraft using the ranges, its radar equipment being updated with new Decca built apparatus 5 years later. For additional radar assistance for high level work and descent to and climb from the ranges, where it was necessary to deconflict with civilian aircraft, the powerful air defence and military air traffic control radar at RAF Sopley, near Hurn, was used in conjunction with the mobile unit. Meanwhile in July 1952 the ranges were closed on the 9th to allow MGM camera crews to shoot footage for the forthcoming film 'The Dambusters'. Some of the most impressive, for their day, aircraft to use the ranges were the Boeing B-29 Washingtons, which served with the RAF from 1950 to 1954 as stop-gap heavy bombers whilst the Service

Chesil Bank Range. Completed 'just in time to be closed down'! The shoreside lookout and triangulation building, adjacent to the Sea Camp Holiday Camp, at Fleet is now a holiday home.

awaited the introduction into service of the V-bombers.

On 3 September 1959 HQ Bomber Command issued a signal stating that the range, in its current form would close at midnight on 11 October and today the Lyme Bay Ranges (as they are now known) – together with the Wembury and Portland Ranges – come under the control of Plymouth Military Radar, with danger area EG D012 having geographic limits very similar to the former Chesil Bank Bombing and Gunnery Ranges area. The overall picture today is shown in this table:

Danger Area Designator	Vertical Limits	Activities Normally Carried Out
EG D012	Surface level up to 18,000', with occasional activity up to 25,000'.	Air Firing and Bombing.
EG D013	Surface level up to 60,000'.	Air Firing, Bombing, Pilotless Target Aircraft and Ship Exercises.
EG D014	Surface level up to 5,000', with occasional activity up to 15,000'.	Bombing, Missile Firing and Ship Exercises.
EG D017	Surface level up to 22,000', with occasional activity up to 55,000'.	Pilotless Target Aircraft, Firing and Ship Exercises.

Today the Chesil itself is no longer a target, but these waters, and the airspace above them, still echo to the sounds of the RAF in Dorset. The spirit and skills of the pilots and weapons system officers and operators of the twenty-first century (the terms navigator, air signaller, flight engineer and the like no longer feature in modern RAF terminology) mirror those of the aircrews who practised here in their parents and grandparents' days: Typhoon, through air defence variant Tornado, has replaced Spitfire; Nimrod, through Shackleton, replaced Sunderland and Liberator; Hercules, through York and Hastings, has replaced Dakota; and attack variant Tornado, through Vulcan and Victor, has replaced Lancaster and Halifax. The ethos, though, is just the same.

For details of the airstrip at Chickerell please see the Airfields chapter.

BALLARD DOWN

The beautiful area of cliff top and headland between the resort town of Swanage and the village of Studland, with dramatic views across the Channel towards the Isle of Wight, is known as Ballard Down. In Victorian times it boasted a rifle range, but during the period 1943 to 1944 the down was used for a different type of military activity: it was the site of an air-to-ground gunnery range.

It was readily apparent to the planning teams formulating policy for Operation Overlord that the German Wehrmacht would possess superiority over the Allied ground forces in armoured fighting vehicles and that the only effective way of neutralising this superiority was by the use of air power. For the RAF this meant the Hawker Typhoon aircraft, which had been designed to replace the Hurricane as an interceptor, but lacked sufficient performance above about 20,000 feet and went on to forge its own place in the RAF's inventory as a ground attack aircraft. Thus it was on this formidable aircraft which pounded the targets on Ballard Down, and similar sites elsewhere, that the pilots honed their skills and later wrought such unimaginable carnage in the Falaise Gap in August 1944.

SIX

THE ROYAL AIR FORCE ON THE WATER

THE AIR SEA RESCUE UNITS

Of the three RAF Air Sea Rescue units based in the county, the one established at Lyme Regis saw by far the longest period of service.

No 30 ASRMCU

This Marine Craft Unit, which opened in 1937, was initially established to provide support to the Chesil Beach Bombing and Gunnery Ranges, the main tasks allocated being the carrying out of range clearance procedures (to ensure that it was safe for the aircraft using the range and that there were no fishing boats or other craft impinging it), to provide target facilities (either with the dedicated target boat or by towing a target) and to provide a rescue service to any aircraft in trouble in the area. On the outbreak of war the unit, which was to be numbered No 37 Air Sea Rescue and Marine Craft Unit from 1942, was ideally positioned to provide an ASR service off the western Dorset coastline.

The craft in use at that time for range duties were not particularly seaworthy – certainly not for deep water rescues – so the launches then in use were supplemented by the Belgian rescue craft *Ministre Lippens*. A sturdy clinker-built vessel, her main limitations were that of having a maximum speed of only 6 to 7

A RAF 68 foot High Speed Rescue and Target Towing Vessel off the Dorset coast.

An Air Sea Rescue craft ashore at Lyme Regis, probably in 1940.

knots and not being fitted with a cabin. She served at Lyme Regis on and off during the war years and was later re-engined in an attempt to improve her performance, which pretty much mirrored that of the RNLI's lifeboats at that time, hull design seeing speed being sacrificed for stability.

The shallow waters inside the Cobb in Lyme Regis harbour had two major effects on the unit: until the late 1950s instead of having the more typical high speed launches used for rescue work, 37 ASRMCU was equipped with seaplane tenders which drew much less water, and secondly it was necessary to keep the 'duty boats' on moorings mid-harbour to ensure that they could put to sea if there was a 'crash call'. The row out to these moorings in a rough sea and, perhaps, in the middle of the night, was far from being a pleasant experience! A local wartime enhancement carried out to the launches was the fitting of twin Browning machine guns to a beam installed across the aft decks.

Worthy of comment is the target boat A356, based at the unit until 1940 when she was shipped out to Canada. She was built with a strong triple skinned mahogany hull, so instead of planning to hit a static or towed target with their practice bombs, pilots were actually briefed to try and actually hit her. Her crew members were paid an additional 1/- (5p) per day-at-sea danger money, and in the event of a direct hit and the noise of it disabling or disorienting the crew a dead man's handle came into play to throttle back her 100 hp engines and allowed a gyro device to put her twin rudders to full deflection until the chase vessel could come alongside, shut down the engines and replace the crew. Of course the vast number of practice bombs dropping into Lyme Bay had a devastating effect on

The two Polish airmen after their rescue by the *Ministre Lippens* (on the right) on the Cobb at Lyme Regis in July 1942.

the fish and the unit personnel would bring large catches of stunned fish ashore to supplement the rations at RAF Warmwell as well as in the cookhouse at Lyme Regis. In October 1943 a second armoured target boat saw service at the unit.

Posted in to command the unit on 3 February 1942 was the 'larger than life' character Flight Lieutenant Sir Algeron Guinness, a member of the famous brewing family and easily recognised as he made his way around the town – petrol permitting – in his distinctive Lagonda car. Although he reputedly never went to sea in any of the vessels under his command, he was very aware of the limitations under which his crews operated and set immediately about acquiring better vessels, being rewarded when ST1506 was delivered directly from her British Powerboat Company manufacturer on 11 May 1942. At 41' 6' long (12.6 m) and of shallow draft, she was the ideal boat for the unit.

Although not as busy as some of the ASRMCUs based along the North Sea and Dover Straits coastlines, No 37 saw its fair share of action, with a total of 65 lives being saved during the war years alone. For example, in the summer of 1940 two crew members (out of 5 onboard) were rescued from a Luftwaffe Heinkel III, in April 1942 the crew was rescued from a Halifax bomber of 10 Sqn which ditched 8 miles off Lyme Regis by the crew of ST480 and three months later the two Polish crew members of a Beaufighter of 307 Sqn based at RAF Exeter were plucked from the water by the crew of *Ministre Lippens*. In August 1943 launch ST480 proceeded to sea to save the two man crew of a 151 Sqn Mosquito from RAF Middle Wallop, and on the evening of D-Day the crew of ST1506 (which had been stationed off Portland Bill for just such an eventuality) rescued 14 people from a Horsa glider which had broken its tow and come down in the sea in mid-Channel. Two further rescues in June 1944 were the seven man crew of a Warwick aircraft, itself involved in ASR operations, by ST305, and the nine members of a USAAF Fortress crew by ST1506.

With the cessation of hostilities in Europe the unit's workload reduced – but not for long. The RAF's participation in the Korean War, 1950 to 1953, the Suez debacle of 1956 and the long-running international aggravation of the Cold War, the origins of which can be traced back prior to the blockade of Berlin from June 1948 to May 1949, all necessitated the RAF and Fleet Air Arm wishing to train on the ranges. The working routine was for the duty boat to be in position off Wyke Regis/Chickerell by 0600 hours each morning that the ranges were active, with a second crew taking over the duty in the afternoon. Post-war the unit strength was normally between 30 and 35 personnel.

On 31 October 1952 the duty boat was scrambled to rescue the RN pilot of Sea Fury T2 VX297 which ditched off Lyme Regis's East Beach following an engine failure – the pilot, Lieutenant Commander D. Montagu being safely brought ashore. On 11th November 1960 a response of a different kind was called for when a Meteor T7 WF766 from Boscombe Down crashed three miles north west of the town at Trinity Hill and personnel from the unit rushed to the scene in the unit's 3 ton truck. Sadly on this occasion the pilot did not survive.

With the introduction of Search and Rescue helicopters into RAF service with 22 and 202 Sqns (note the change in terminology from ASR to SAR) in the mid-1950s, the emphasis changed from launches to rotary wing aircraft for the rescue of downed aircrew at sea, and reflecting this the unit was at this time redesignated as No 1111 Marine Craft Unit. During this phase of its operational life the unit was involved in numerous trails sponsored by the Aircraft and Armament Experimental Establishment at Boscombe Down – and not always working on things that were designed to go off with a bang. Sonobuoys, life jacket personal locater beacons, and ejector seat trials were amongst these more peaceful activities.

The unit soldiered on until closure in July 1964, civilianisation and helicopters having rapidly established themselves as the way forward. The unit was always a happy, but hard working one, and in July 1994 many of those who had served afloat and ashore at Lyme Regis gathered in the town for a major reunion. Today the headquarters building is in commercial use (with a commemorative plaque on its wall), the boat yard is a car park and the slipway used to bring vessels ashore for maintenance and repair can still be seen adjacent to the RNLI boathouse, where a modern Atlantic 75 class inshore rescue boat *Pearl of Dorset* continues the rescue tradition at Lyme Regis.

No 40 ASRMCU

The second Air Sea Rescue unit in the county, No 40 ASRMCU, was formed at Weymouth on 6 April 1944 under the command of Flt Lt W. G. Howes. The unit's first two marine craft, High Speed Launches 2696 and 2697, arrived at Weymouth from Dover on 20 April with HSL2694 arriving in the port the next day. The unit was declared operational on 27 April, with the crews initially sleeping aboard their vessels, but messing with the Royal Navy at HMS *Grasshopper* – Weymouth

Naval Base, with its headquarters in the 'closed for the duration' Pavilion Theatre. The messing arrangements proved impracticable, so rations were drawn instead (from the Portland naval base HMS *Osprey*) and then cooked on the boats – it was probably administratively inconvenient as much as anything else to do otherwise, for on 28 April HMS *Grasshopper* had been handed over to the US Navy as local preparations for D-Day intensified. Later on the off duty personnel were messed and accommodated at the domestic site at Chickerell airfield; for at least part of the time that it was operational, the unit's headquarters and operations room was in the old Customs House building, now the home of 'Portland Coastguard'. Refuelling was normally carried out within the confines of Portland Harbour rather than alongside at Weymouth, and boats which need to be hauled out of the water for maintenance or repair used the Great Western railway slipway adjacent to the Weymouth Lifeboat station.

The unit's first 'crash calls' were on 7 (2 calls) and 24 May, but all three searches were abortive – although they gave the crews the opportunity of working together under operational conditions.

On D-Day itself Weymouth launches were positioned offshore ready to assist any casualties from the massive air armada flying overhead. Unfortunately, the pre-positioning of the boats seems not to have been known to all whom it should have been – for at just after 8.00 am HSLs 2691 and 2697 were attacked by six Beaufighter aircraft to the south of St Aldhelm's Head. Fortunately, this 'Blue on Blue' incident did little damage to the launches!

The following day four injured US airmen were brought ashore from *HMS Skate*; then, on the 11th, 40 ASRMCU carried out its first actual rescue, one airmen being rescued by HSL2691 – with sister ship 2697 finding only two empty life rafts at the same place. The rest of June was equally busy, aircraft related incidents including:

June 11: HSL2707 took a Mustang pilot off a destroyer south of Portland Bill and landed him at Portland.

The crew of HSL2696 spotted an aircraft in obvious difficulties before it ditched, but only one survivor was found despite the prompt response.

June 12: HSL2696 proceeded to a reported crash 5 miles north east of Portland Bill, picked up the pilot and landed him at Portland.

June 22: HSL2697, with 2696 in support, towed a Walrus flying boat to Portland which had carried out a landing in Weymouth Bay and had then become fouled on the anchor cable of a landing craft. Aboard the aircraft were its three crew and a single survivor who had earlier been rescued by the Walrus.

Both of the noteworthy events which occurred in July 1944 involved HSL2694. On the 20th she put to sea to take nine survivors off *HMCS Q'Appelle* – the survivors being crew members of *US Tug 75*, which had become lost in fog off the Channel Islands and come under gunfire from the German coastal defence

Hostilities over, 3 of the Weymouth-based ASR launches lie alongside the Harbour's Customs House Quay before reassignment in October 1945. The paddle steamer in the foreground is the PS *Embassy*, recently returned to her home port after war service as HMS *Ambassador*.

batteries on Alderney. Four days later, on 24 July 1944, the Unit Diary records that the crew of the same launch recovered the body of a Flying Officer Ollett, which they came across whilst searching for another aircraft – the crew of which was rescued by a Walrus. The only Ollett recorded as losing his life at about this time in the war was Flying Officer James Frederick Ollett of No 179 Squadron, a unit flying both Warwick V and Lancaster ASR3 aircraft in the air sea rescue role.

On 3 October Pinnace 78 rescued the two crew members of a Barracuda aircraft, which had ditched just off Portland Harbour's Breakwater Fort. They were both uninjured and, after being landed at Weymouth, were taken to RAF Warmwell by ambulance.

By November 1944, the original launches at the unit had all gone, having been replaced by three 63' 'Whaleback' HSLs – 184 (Captain: Flying Officer Jones), 185 (Flight Lieutenant Farr), and 168 (Flying Officer Crosby). The unit strength was 4 officers and 54 NCOs and airmen.

After a quiet start to 1945 (with just one call out, responded to by HSL185, on 23 March for the crew of a Beaufighter aircraft which crashed on the Chesil Beach ranges), one of the most unusual call outs received by the unit came on 6 July – Weymouth being involved as the No 36 ASRMCU at Poole had by now been stood down. An American Navy PBY Catalina flying boat was reported down in the sea some seven miles south east of Bournemouth with engine trouble, and HSL2509 was scrambled to the scene. Both of the PBY's engines had run out of oil. A Noorduyn Norseman aircraft, almost certainly an American one, as those allocated to the RAF under Lend-Lease seem all to have been retained in Canada, dropped drums of oil to the stranded flying boat and 2509 herself passed across two 15 gallon drums of oil. The sumps topped up, the Pratt & Whitney Twin Wasp radial piston engines were restarted and the PBY taxied into Poole Harbour

A flotilla of Wheeler class U S Coastguard rescue cutters were based at Poole from shortly before D-Day until the end of 1944, saving 1,438 lives.

escorted by the RAF launch.

This was the last life-saving/productive service by 40 ASRMCU, although the final call out came on 6 August when an aircraft crashed near No 1 Target off Chesil Beach – but the pilot's body was recovered by a local fishing boat before the HSL arrived on scene.

After VE Day, by which time the unit was under the command of Flying Officer, later Flight Lieutenant, Terry, it became the practice for one of the Weymouth vessels to be detached to the Channel Islands on a weekly rotation.

The final vessels allocated to the unit were LRRC 014 and 015 which were conversions of Fairmile motor torpedo/gun boats, and it was these two modern rescue craft, with occasional relief vessels, which continued to serve at Weymouth until the unit's disbandment on 15 June 1946, coincidentally the same day that the ferry service from Weymouth to The Channel Islands resumed after the war cessation – the *St Helier* (Captain R. R. Pitman), a proud veteran of the Dunkirk evacuation of June 1940, sailing from the port that same Saturday evening.

On closure the units tally board showed that it had directly rescued 11 downed aircrew and brought ashore 99 survivors from other vessels that had already rescued them.

No 36 ASRMCU

No 36 ASRMCU was the third of Dorset's Air Sea Rescue units. It was established in Poole Harbour, its base being at Salternes Pier, and scheduled to become operational on 17 April 1944. However some three weeks or so before this date at least one of the unit's boats had been in action, as on 25 March 36 ASRMCU is credited with the rescue of 24 personnel from a locally ditched glider. This could possibly have been by one of the vessels taken over by the Senior Naval Officer Poole prior to the RAF unit's activation as a rescue service for any pilot having to ditch in the Poole or Swanage area. Records show that *B015 Eve, B050*

Just as the RAF's Search and Rescue helicopters of 22 and 202 Squadrons co-operate with the RNLI's lifeboats today, so did the ASR aircraft co-operate with the marine craft of an earlier generation. Here a Westland Lysander aircraft of No 277 Squadron, probably at RAF Hurn, is loaded with its air-droppable liferafts prior to a sortie.

Commodore and simply *B029* were the vessels requisitioned, with *Eve* being of particular use in heavy seas. The speedboats *Speedlark IX* and *Speedlark X*, capable of 25 knots in calmer conditions, from the Bolson boatyard could also be called upon if necessary.

A particularly noteworthy rescue was that carried out on 2 June when the crew of a ditched Walrus aircraft was picked up just 10 miles off the enemy occupied coast off Cherbourg. Weather permitting and in addition to the 'alert' boat alongside at Salternes Pier, it was common practice to station one vessel off Durlston Head – where co-incidentally RAF Tilly Whim was sited – to reduce response time in the event of a 'crash call' being initiated. In the pre-RAF days *Eve* was often stationed there.

The base closed down on 7 November 1944. There is no doubt that this small RAF unit would have been massively outsized by Rescue Flotilla One of the US Coastguard, which based 60 Wheeler 83' (25.3 m) rescue cutters at Poole from spring to December 1944 and during which time saved 1,438 lives.

The standard colour scheme for the vessels at all three RAF units was one of a black hull (above the anti-fouling), and grey decks and superstructure, with an RAF roundel on either side of the bows immediately ahead of the pennant number, which was also painted on the stern. A larger roundel was usually painted on the foredeck to assist in identification from the air. Until the fitting of air band VHF radios became widespread on the boats a red and white chequer pattern was painted on those so equipped.

In addition to the vessels associated with the county's three Air Sea Rescue units, which all included humble general duties tenders as well as the impressive rescue launches themselves, the RAF was 'on the water' in Dorset in two other guises: supporting the operational flying boats of RAF Hamworthy in Poole

... but a humble rowing boat – yet a vital component in maintaining flying boats afloat on the trots in Poole Harbour. 'Chiefie' sits in the bow, whilst the mascot Airedale terrier maintains lookout from the stern.

Harbour and carrying out maintenance work in association with the target buoys moored in Lyme Bay for the Chesil Beach Bombing and Gunnery Ranges.

FLYING BOAT SUPPORT VESSELS

Unless a flying boat was ashore on its beaching legs, all transits to and from the aircraft had to be across the water, so to achieve this RAF Hamworthy, in common with all flying boat bases, had a variety of small vessels provided for the engineers to enable them to carry out their duties. These boats were either purpose built for task or, in many cases, commandeered locally and included refuelling bowsers, control launches, crash boats and general purpose vessels for carrying crews to and from their aircraft and also for ensuring that the water runway was clear of floating debris during flying operations. One task undertaken which was exclusive to flying boat operations was that of, on a calm day, creating wakes at 90 degrees to the aircraft's intended take-off path to allow the hull to break the friction with the water's surface and allow the aircraft to become airborne.

RAF RANGE SUPPORT AND LIFTING VESSELS

Nationally the RAF possessed 16 of these ships over the years, none purpose-built for the job, and the six that worked locally were the RAFV *Rafmoor* (172 gross tons), RAFV *Rangemoor* (351 tons), RAFV *Airmoor* (177 tons), RAFV *Mainmoor*, RAFV *Salmoor* (178 tons) and RAFV *Watchmoor* (139 tons), using Weymouth Harbour as their base.

The vessels' main tasks were to carry maintenance parties out to the buoys for routine jobs such as painting, minor repairs from practice bomb and inert shell damage and the occasional change of the bulbs in the flashing lights that the targets were fitted with and, secondly, to bring the rafts ashore for deep maintenance or heavy repair work. In this latter case the rafts were brought to a slip at Ferrybridge, accessed via Portland Harbour, but occasionally could be seen moored alongside at Weymouth whilst fair weather was awaited before the raft was towed around the wild waters off Portland Bill to be re-sited on the range.

Although the ranges ceased to be controlled locally in October 1959 the mooring vessels continued to tie up at Weymouth well into the 1960s, whilst as late as the 1980s the former *Mainmoor* could be seen plying her trade in Newport Docks under her new name *Buoymoor*.

RAFV *Salmoor* in Hope Cove, Weymouth, in the early 1950s and RAFV *Rangemoor* alongside Weymouth Harbour's North Quay about 10 years later.

SEVEN

BARRAGE BALLOONS

One important but unglamorous function of the RAF in the county during the Second World War was the provision of barrage balloons in areas with high value targets, with many of those handling the enormous balloons – nicknamed 'Big Berthas' – being members of the WAAF. The balloons, partially filled with hydrogen gas, were tethered to their control winches by cables, with each balloon being crewed by about ten airmen/airwomen, normally under the command of a corporal.

A barrage balloon being prepared for raising and, below, deployed. A couple of points of interest are the winch to the rear of the grounded balloon and the fact that the balloons were not rigid, the slight 'slackness' improving their stability.

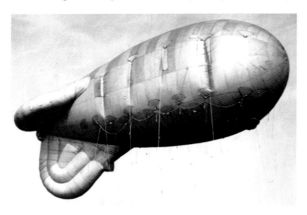

In addition to the tethering cable, other metal cables hung from the balloons – the overall aim being to bring down or deter low flying enemy aircraft.

Barrage balloons were used throughout the years of the Second World War, but by far the greatest concentration present in Dorset was over the D-Day period. The local headquarters of No 997 (Balloon) Squadron, a mobile unit specifically tasked with the defence of ports, was in Rodwell Road, Weymouth, and it oversaw detachments at Poole (No 112 Flight) and Weymouth/Portland (No 111 and No 113 Flights) from April until July 1944, after which the majority of the squadron moved away to Gravesend as part of the south-east's defences against the V-1 flying bombs.

EIGHT

DECOY SITES

The Decoy Site on what is now the golf course at the Moors Valley Leisure Park at Three Legged Cross was one of two set up to decoy enemy aircraft away from the fighter airfield at RAF Ibsley, just across the county boundary near Ringwood in Hampshire. The other was at Woodgreen, near Fordingbridge. Its location was such that it was also considered as a decoy for RAF Hurn, which itself had a second decoy located on Ridley Plain in the New Forest.

The one at Three Legged Cross consisted of an above ground concrete bunker divided into two main rooms, one for the lighting controls, telephone line to its controlling authority and the very basics of comfort and the second housing a generator and associated fume extraction ducting. The entrance doors were protected by blast walls.

The decoy itself, known as a 'Q site and designed for use at night only, consisted of a line of parallel lights laid out to look from above like a runway, together with the mixture of red obstruction lights and the like that would be seen at an aerodrome conducting night flying. It was manned by a small team of RAF personnel who were billeted in nearby Verwood and it remained operational until the war's end.

Altogether there were 839 decoy sites throughout the country during the Second World War, the only other RAF site was that on Knighton Heath, a decoy for RAF Warmwell. Positioned some three and a half miles south-east of the airfield, the site is now occupied by the Winfrith Technology Park and the decommissioned Winfrith Nuclear Energy site.

The Three Legged Cross decoy control bunker as it is today. It can be found by the 9th green at Moors Valley Leisure Park Golf Club

NINE

THE ROYAL OBSERVER CORPS

The Royal Observer Corps (ROC), initially the Observer Corps, can trace its origins way back to the pre-radar days of 1916 when the Metropolitan Observation Service, under Army control, was formed to report on German Zeppelin airships and Gotha and Staaken bombers in the London area. By 1924 it was becoming increasingly obvious to the Air Ministry that it needed a national system to locate enemy aircraft, and this led to the formation of the Observer Corps the following year. Control of the new organisation was transferred from the Army to the RAF in 1929, thus earning it a place in our story, and had become a vital part of the nation's air defence system by the time that war broke out in the autumn of 1939.

The task of the observers was to supplement the electronic picture provided by the radar stations, which were not only unable to identify the types of aircraft being detected or count precisely the number of targets, but were almost totally ineffective after enemy raiders had 'coasted in' and were lost from the radar screens in ground returns and clutter.

Reporting posts, the vast majority of which became operational in September 1938, reported directly to Group Centres which then passed the reported information on to the Fighter Group operations rooms, and during the Battle of Britain, when the clear summer skies helped visual observation, the sightings from the Corps' posts proved to be invaluable. This, in Churchillian terms, 'was their finest hour'. The Corps was honoured with the royal recognition in April 1941 and was henceforth the Royal Observer Corps.

One little known aspect of its work was the invaluable role it played in locating and guiding to safety those aircraft which were damaged or off-course, with a further development being a ground-to-air H/F radio system named 'Darky' used to assist Allied aircraft in difficulties. Nationally some 7,000 aircraft were saved by ROC intervention and a further 1,800 damaged ones assisted to a safe landing. Some posts were also equipped with a system codenamed 'Totter', which were rocket flares which could be fired off to indicate to friendly forces the positions of enemy aircraft or V1 'doodlebug' rockets.

The ROC didn't stand down until four days after VE Day, its lookouts being manned in case of a renegade attack by German aircraft, only to be reactivated in January 1947 when it became clear that war with the Soviet Union was a true possibility. The ROC continued to fulfil its visual observation task until 1965, but with aircraft now capable of flying twice as high and three times as fast as early post-war aircraft,

ABOVE The Poundbury Observer Corps post in winter.

RIGHT With both Hot and Cold War memories, Worth Matravers post in 2009.

and airborne early warning and command and control aircraft such as the Boeing AWACS Sentry in service, the final 280 surface posts were closed.

Earlier than this though, from 1957, the ROC had started to be tasked in a second role – that of reporting and monitoring the after-effects of radioactive fallout after a nuclear attack by the Soviet Union, the old surface observation posts being replaced by some 1,562 underground posts, of which 19 were in Dorset. The observers had simple instruments to measure blast yield, the height and angle of flash from nuclear explosions, and the short-lived but lethal radiation from weapons fallout, but thankfully their skills were never put to the test. In 1991, following the ending of the Cold War in 1989, the ROC was stood down.

The 21 wartime Dorset posts were at Abbotsbury, Bere Regis, Blandford Forum, Bridport, Buckland Newton, Canford Cliffs, Christchurch, Fontwell Magna, Foreland (near Old Harry Rocks), Gillingham, Maiden Newton, Portland Bill, Poundbury, Preston, Sturminster Newton, Verwood, Wareham, West Lulworth, Wimborne Minster/Broadstone, Worth Matravers and Yetminster. Of these only Foreland closed before the general stand down, although the Bridport, Gillingham, Maiden Newton and Wimborne Minster/Broadstone posts were relocated to more suitable sites for nuclear reporting, taking the new names Burton Bradstock, East Stour, Evershot and Witchampton respectively.

TEN

MEMORIALS

The vast majority of the graves of military personnel in the county are maintained by the Commonwealth War Graves Commission with, of course, Royal Air Force headstones standing proud within rows of varying lengths alongside their fallen comrades in arms. There are too many of these scattered final resting places for us to list them all, but here are just a representative few.

THE PURBECK AIR CRASHES MEMORIAL SEAT

Located on the edge of Polar Wood in the Purbeck Hills above the village of Kingston, this seat, dedicated in October 2007, remembers those who died at this spot in two separate air crashes: a Fairey Swordfish Mk I of the Torpedo Training Unit at RAF Gosport on 18 March 1938 and a Consolidated Liberator Mk IX of No 232 Squadron, departing RAF Holmsley South in the New Forest, on 15 June 1945.

There were three fatalities in the Swordfish crash and 27 in the Liberator, making the latter the county's worst ever air crash.

The Purbeck Air Crashes Memorial Seat. The memorial can be accessed west of Kingston on the footpath to Swyre Head.

WARMWELL CHURCH

Perhaps the most evocative graveyard from an RAF point of view is this one – at Holy Trinity Church in the village of Warmwell, where there are 21 RAF and Commonwealth Air Forces burials, 2 of whom are unidentified, one soldier (who was killed in an air raid at RAF Warmwell) and a Polish airman. All save one of the headstones commemorates a Second World War casualty, the exception being that of Acting Pilot Officer Adam de Pencier, the son of the then Archbishop of New Westminster, British Columbia, who was killed in a flying accident on the Chesil Bank ranges on 13 March 1939.

THE SHEPHARD MEMORIAL

The Shephard Memorial, is the oldest military aviation memorial in the county. Informal in concept, being in the form of a propeller and hand-painted dedication, it is located in the grounds of Shortlake House at Osmington, Weymouth. Brigadier General Gordon Strachy Shephard DSO, MC, RFC was, at the age of just 32, the youngest officer of such rank in the British Army and was considered to be an outstanding leader, still flying reconnaissance flights over enemy lines himself and renowned for leaving his desk to go into the field and meet face to face

the frontline aircrew under his command. Almost certainly destined for even higher, maybe political, office he was killed in a non-combat flying accident on 19 January 1918 at Auchel in the Nord Pas de Calais, aged 32, and lies buried in the Lapugnoy Military Cemetery near to where he made his last fateful flight.

PILOT OFFICER ALLEN MEMORIAL STONE

At a spot known as Field Grove, part of the Durweston Forest to the west of Blandford Forum, can be found a simple granite memorial stone bearing two plaques: the slightly larger plaque commemorates 19-year-old Pilot Officer John Allen, a Spitfire pilot with No 152 Squadron who crashed near here on 29 November 1940 after, it is thought, a failure of his aircraft's oxygen system, whilst the smaller recalls his father, who also served in the RAF and asked to be remembered with his son who so sadly predeceased him.

PILOT HIGHT ROAD

Early on the evening of 15 August 1940 Supermarine Spitfire Mk I R6988 was shot down by enemy fighters whilst on bomber escort duty and crashed within the borough of Bournemouth. The pilot was a Pilot Officer Cecil Hight of No 234 Squadron based at RAF Middle Wallop, a 22-year-old New Zealander from the North Island town of Stratford, who baled out from his stricken aircraft only for his parachute to fail to open. Maybe it had been damaged in the combat; maybe he was too severely wounded to pull his D-ring – we will now never know.

Cecil Hight is one of the 20 Second World War RAF casualties buried in the Bournemouth East cemetery and is commemorated in the Bournemouth Roman Catholic Cathedral by a plaque of wings made in his memory by his school chums and, rather unusually, by having a road in the town named after him.

THE RHODES-MOORHOUSE MEMORIAL.

This memorial, located on private ground to the rear of Parnham House, Beaminster, is out of the ordinary in that it spans two wars and commemorates father and son. Father was Second Lieutenant William Barnard Rhodes-Moorhouse VC, who was the first airman to be awarded the Victoria Cross which he was posthumously awarded for his bravery on 26 April 1915 when, badly wounded and bleeding

William Rhodes-Moorhouse VC.

heavily, he flew his aircraft back to Allied lines in order to deliver his mission report. He died of his injuries the following day.

The son, Flight Lieutenant William Henry Rhodes-Moorhouse DFC, flew Hurricane aircraft with No 601 (County of London) Squadron in both The Battle of France and The Battle of Britain and with well over five aircraft kills to his credit was an official 'fighter ace'. His good fortune ran out on the morning of 6 September 1940 in the skies over Kent, when he was shot down by a Luftwaffe Me 109 and is justly remembered with his father in the plot at their, then, family home.

OTHER MEMORIALS

It is likely that the memorial plaque in Moreton Churchyard remembering Sergeant Basil Elles Sharp Knowles of 37 Sqn, who died on 1 May 1940 aged 19, and who was known by his family as 'Bill', is amongst the most often viewed, for it is sited immediately behind the headstone of none other than T.E. Lawrence (of Arabia), who incidentally also served in the Air Force under the

name of Ross for much of the period between 1923 and his death in 1935.

The plaque to Sergeant Knowles has been placed within the borders of the grave of his parents, but he, though, has no known resting place and is listed on the Royal Air Forces Memorial at Runnymede, which is beautifully located on a hill overlooking the River Thames above the site of the 1215 signing of the Magna Carta. Knowles was a crew member of a Vickers Wellington bomber participating in Operation Archery, the unsuccessful attempt to prevent the Nazi forces from occupying Norway.

In the Bournemouth, Poole and Christchurch conurbation there are 13 cemeteries with 'RAF' graves or commemorations: 6 from the RFC, 10 from the First World War, 93 from the Second World War and 5 post-war graves. In the north of the county two graveyards at Shaftesbury contain just 2 RAF graves, one from each of the twentieth century wars, whilst there are 5 1939-1945 RAF graves to the west of the county at Lyme Regis. The county town of Dorchester has a single RFC grave, no graves from the First World War but 10 RAF graves from the Second and a single post-war headstone, whilst to the south in Weymouth and Portland lie a single casualty from the First World War and nine from the Second. In Portland's Royal Naval Cemetery lie the mortal remains of 12 German airmen.

ELEVEN

THE FINAL YEARS

The last readily visible RAF presence in Dorset was that associated with the Portland Rotor Radar Station which, as we have seen, ceased to be operational towards the end of the summer of 1956 but, in addition to the RAF Careers establishments and the Air Cadet units in the county, there continued to be two exchange posts for RAF officers at HMS *Osprey*, Portland, until its split closures: an officer attached to the staff of Flag Officer Sea Training (FOST) until March 1995 and an air traffic controller at the helicopter airfield until February 1999.

The base at Portland was mainly dedicated to the bringing to full operational effectiveness warships of the Royal Navy and many of our NATO allies and the officer on FOST's staff, a squadron leader post, had the task of providing professional advice to other members of the FOST team on RAF and NATO maritime patrol and maritime attack aircraft tactics and capabilities, and equally to assist directly in the training and testing of crews going through their work-up procedures. From the UK the RAF aircraft associated with the maritime patrol skills would have been the Avro Shackleton and later the BAE Nimrod, whilst the maritime attack skills would have been exercised by the crews of the Buccaneer and later the Tornado.

Shoreside the RAF provided maritime air inputs in the classroom and then in training scenarios. From 1990 the RAF Staff Officer (RAFSO) provided a major input into Portland-based Area Capability Training, which in itself was absorbed into the much larger Joint Maritime Courses. Almost every Thursday a series of exercises took place in the Portland Training Areas – known locally as 'The Thursday War' – and the RAFSO would be amongst the 'sea riders' accompanying the warships to sea in Weymouth Bay and West Bay (The Portland Danger Areas) to assess

'RAF Sea Rider': Squadron Leader Peter Jones, the last RAF Staff Officer to serve with Flag Officer Sea Training at Portland, at sea on board the Duke Class Type 23 Frigate HMS *Norfolk*.

Today, there are 12 squadrons of Air Cadets based around the county. The photograph on the left shows the No 2185 (Wareham) Squadron march past on Remembrance Sunday. Their training aircraft include Viking T1 gliders (*above*) and Grob T1 Tutors (*below*).

reactions by the ships' staffs to simulated hostile air activity, often provided by the Falcon 20s of Flight Refuelling Ltd and the Hawks of No 100 Squadron. RAF Nimrods would also sometimes be involved in the exercises – which if involving submarines were known as Casexes – with the arranging of the air assets being the job of the RAFSO. FOST is now located at HMS *Drake*, Plymouth, with an ongoing input from the RAF.

Iconic battlefield support helicopter: Boeing Chinook HC1 helicopter in Dorset skies.

The second permanent RAF post at HMS *Osprey* was that of an air traffic control officer (ATCO), working in either the visual control room atop the control tower, itself located on the roof of the 1906 naval canteen, or at the radar screens in the approach control room on the next floor down. The job was certainly a little different from the run of the mill RAF ATC job, for the airstrip had full approach lighting at both ends, precision radar talk down to both ends – but only a useable length of 751 feet (229 meters). Today the Agusta Westland AW139 helicopter of HM Coastguard flies from the former RN airstrip, but is housed in a new hangar on the north side of the runway.

Today there are only two permanent RAF presences in the county: Careers Information and Air Cadets. Over recent years, as the size of our Armed Forces has reduced, the number of Careers Information Offices – we once knew them as Recruiting Centres – has been reduced to one, and this itself is a joint office shared with personnel from the Royal Navy and the Army in Bournemouth's Holdenhurst Road. The staff there does not however confine itself to the office, but can be regularly seen spreading its message at a wide variety of events and locations throughout Dorset, from school open days to carnivals and from air shows to country fairs. Each summer, keeping itself in the public eye, the RAF sponsors a Volleyball Classic on Weymouth's golden sands, which attracts top teams from throughout the British Isles and from continental Europe.

The county's Air Cadet presence is divided between the Air Training Corps (ATC) and the RAF sections of Combined Cadet Force units (CCF [RAF]). The ATC units are town-based, with twelve squadrons spread around the county, two of which have their own detached flights, whilst the four CCF (RAF) units are school-based, but both have a common ethos of helping youngsters from the age of 13 to 19 participate in a wide range of activities, not all by any means directly aviation associated. As well as gliding and power flying, cadets are encouraged to help out in their local communities and participate in the Duke of Edinburgh Award scheme. Nationwide there are over 60,000 cadets, the Volunteer Gliding Schools form the largest gliding organisation in the country and the Air Cadets provide the largest number of entrants from a single youth organisation in the Duke of Edinburgh Award scheme.

In this second decade of the twenty-first century RAF air defence and air traffic control radars still silently sweep the airspace above us, but from distant locations, and only by looking to the skies can we see operational RAF activity in Dorset. The most obvious, of course, is the world famous Red Arrows Aerobatic Team with its 'nine ship' Hawk aircraft formation, displaying some of the finest flying to be seen internationally, whilst more evocative but less dramatic are the Lancaster, Spitfire and Hurricane trio of the RAF Battle of Britain Memorial Flight. Many a time the fast approaching noise of military jet engines will be followed by the glimpsing site of low flying operational jets, such as the Tornado or Typhoon, or trainers such as the Hawk, Embraer Tucano or Beech King Air B200s, for only by practising their low flying skills can RAF pilots maintain and enhance the combat readiness so important in today's troubled world. Finally, Dorset's skies often see Hercules transports and Chinook helicopters exercising, these often after dark with the pilots using night vision goggles for terrain avoidance, and offshore, until as recently as 2009, the occasional Nimrod might have been spotted, exercising with naval forces, supporting the UK Border Agency or fulfilling the Service's long range search and rescue commitment. Sadly the Nimrod was completely withdrawn from service following the 2010 Defences Security Review and we now are a nation with no 'blue water' maritime patrol aircraft.

The intense activity of the war years is now but a memory, but a memory of which Dorset can be proud. Today there are different foes, different problems and vastly different equipment, but all still aligned with the Royal Air Force's motto 'Per Ardua ad Astra' – through struggles to the stars.

In 'Swan' formation, the longest and widest formation that the Royal Air Force Aerobatic Team flies, the Red Arrows roar over the roof of Weymouth's Pavilion Theatre.

FURTHER READING

Air-Britain Historians, *RAF Flying Training and Support Units Since* 1912 (2007)

Ashworth, N, *The Anzac Squadron* (1994)

Cassidy, B, *Flying Empires* (1996)

Cooke, A, *Airfield Focus 21*: Warmwell (1995)

Dobinson, C, *Fields of Deception* (1970)

Hayward, F & L, *A History of RAF Christchurch 1940-42.* (1998) (Private Work)

Hill, G, *Memories of RAF Christchurch 1940 – 1943* (1997) (Private Work)

Hoodless, W. A, *Hengistbury Head* (2005)

Phipp, M, *Bournemouth's Airfields, A History* (2006)

Pomeroy, C, *The Flying Boats of Bermuda* (2000)

    Military Dorset Today (1995)

    Wings Over Weymouth (2005)

Rimmel, K, *RAF Lyme Regis: Air Sea Rescue Base 1937-64* (Private work)

Smith, G, *Dorset Airfields in the Second World War* (1999)

White, A, *Christchurch Airfield. 40 Years of Flying* (1978)

Ziegler F, *The Story of 609 Squadron* (1971)

ACKNOWLEDGEMENTS

I am grateful to the following for their help with the text and illustrations: Air Commodore Norman Ashworth RAAF, Maureen Attwooll, Aviation Heritage Museum of Western Australia, Jim Bradford, David Bruton, Colin Cruddas, Squadron Leader Mike Dean, Easton Lodge Preservation Trust, Sylvia Ellis, Jim Fail, Aldon Ferguson, Friends of the New Forest Airfields Association, Chris Gannon, Peter Garwood, Lawrence Holmes, The Imperial War Museum, Brian Jackson, Squadron Leader Peter Jones, Gerry Knott, John Leech, John Levesley, Barry Lovett, Lyme Regis Philpot Museum, Mike Phipp, Hugh Mulligan, Norman Pearce, Mike Phipp, Poole Flying Boat Celebration, Purbeck Radar Museum Trust, Frederick Quinn Archive, Red House Museum Christchurch, Robert Rooker, Patrick Rose, Roger Starling, Royal Australian Air Force Department of Defence, Alan E. Smith, No 609 Squadron Association, No 644 Squadron Association, and Bill Voysey.